What's a Southern Belle

Doing in a Place Like This?

Learn how to get out and get happy!

Karri J. McClure

ISBN-13: 978-1-71995-958-2

What's a Southern Belle Doing in a Place Like This? Learn how to get out and get happy by Karri J. McClure Published by Karri J. McClure, Casa Grande, AZ 85193 www.karrijmcclure.com
For permissions contact: www.karrijmcclure.com Cover by Stacy Fife

DEDICATION

I dedicate this book to my brother Kevin. I feel you close
to me, and miss you every day. I will always treasure the
beautiful memories we shared, and remember how you
supported me with unconditional love. Oh how I miss you,
my dear sweet brother.

Love, KJ

TABLE OF CONTENTS

ACKNOWLEDGMENTS

To my parents, thank you for your support and unconditional love. Special thanks to Stacy Fife for designing my beautiful book cover, and for laughing at my crazy, every day. Thank you to Sabrina Larsen for editing my heart's work, and to Carrie Shaw for your weekly calls, and for listening to every podcast and reading every blog that I have created.

Finally, thank you to the people in my life who have made me stronger. The lessons were greatly appreciated.

All you need is faith, trust, and a little pixie dust.

-Tinkerbell

INTRODUCTION

I spent the first twelve years of my life living between two midsize towns in North Carolina. When I say between two towns, I mean out in the middle of nowhere. My address included Rural Route 311, and Richard Petty's daughter-in-law was my kindergarten teacher. If you don't know who Richard Petty is, you aren't Southern enough. I had a mom who worked so hard to put food on the table that she sacrificed her own dreams most of the time, and a daddy who decided he was going to do exactly what he wanted, and it didn't include our family. He walked out the door when I was eight years old.

When my daddy left, being the oldest at home, I took on a lot of responsibilities that included mowing a half-acre lot, and making sure my grandma put her cigarette out before she fell asleep so that she didn't burn the house down. It was my job to keep us safe while my mom worked the night shift at Howard Johnsons. So there I was at eight years old with a missing daddy, a momma who worked all the time, and a grandma who liked bourbon in her iced tea, and could accidentally burn the house down at any moment. None of that added up to more than a really crappy start. I wasn't happy. In fact, I was so miserable that I kept a suitcase packed under my bed so that if I decided to run, I would be ready to go. Looking back, I am pretty sure that suitcase contained a pair of pants, my favorite hand-me-down Barbie doll, and a homemade bed that I had made for her out of Popsicle sticks and cotton balls.

I was ready to run to something better at any given moment, and I actually tried it once. My mom was at work and my sister, my brother, and I were home. I think I was nine and I was damn near fed up. I grabbed my flip flops and my suitcase, and decided to leave in search of happiness because it sure wasn't on Rural Route 311 that day. I pranced out the front door, yelled goodbye forever to my sister, and got half a mile down a very busy road before some semblance of logic kicked in, and I determined that I had nowhere to go. Thinking about the runaway after school specials I had seen, I realized that I was too pretty to end up that way, and I turned around. In that moment, as miserable as I was, I realized I was stuck. So I turned around, walked back to the house, put my packed suitcase under the bed, and sat down. My sister told on me when my mom got home and she yelled. She yelled a lot that day, and although upset at me, I am certain that she wanted to run away from our lives as much as I did. It was the only reality I knew and I was pretty sure God hated me.

So there I sat in the middle of nowhere in North Carolina, wondering if anybody was really happy. Would I ever be happy? If not, what the hell was the point to all this madness? I learned at a very young age that sometimes life isn't good to you. You find yourself in spots that you never imagined you would, and you have no idea how to get to the happiness that you really want. I have looked in the mirror and asked the girl looking back, "What the hell am I doing here?" For a lot of years she didn't know the answer, and I waited in fear and avoidance, and I lied a little about the reality before me. The truth is, at any moment you have the ability to change direction and move toward a better existence. All it takes is a choice to be happy, and with a little dedication and hard work, anything is possible.

I blamed my father for not being the daddy that I really needed. I misunderstood that his choices gave him joy while we suffered. I developed a belief that the amount of happiness in the world was somehow limited, and there wasn't enough for me. That was a myth. There is an abundance of happiness, and all anyone has to do is get out there and find it. Everyone has their own story to tell, and sometimes the story doesn't turn out exactly the way it was planned. Be proud of your story because it makes you who you are.

I spent years blaming my dad for the loss of more than a few childhood opportunities. I assumed that somehow he got all the happiness, and was out living and fulfilling his dreams. I hated him for leaving, and I hated seeing the tears my mom cried when she thought I wasn't watching.

My mother's hard work and dedication paid off, and when I was almost thirteen we moved to Hilton Head Island, in South Carolina. Beaches and palm trees in the salty air became my new reality. You mean to tell me that for the first twelve years of my life, this place existed and people really lived like this? My mom continued to work as hard as she always had, for a man who paid her very well. She made sure that no matter how many hours she had to put in, dinner was made and on the table, and our homework was done at the end of the day. My daddy even came back. He decided that family life was the life for him after all. We were never to mention his absent years. The past was the past, and we were to let it all go. Although that would have put us in a place of blissful avoidance, I was just a little too upset and feisty to do that. We were all going to be miserable, and I did my part to make sure no one forgot. I worked very hard to build a shrine to my lost years and misery. This did not make for a very good relationship with my dad. I was so busy holding onto the pain, and blaming him for everything, that I didn't have time to understand or acknowledge the bigger picture. It wasn't until years later—long after he was gone—that I could look at his life with love, and understand that his choices had nothing to do with me.

My father's first memory in life was chasing a car down the road after being dropped off at an orphanage with his three-month-old brother. His mother had decided that it was better for them to be there than to be under her care, and just as quickly as they arrived at the boy's home, she was gone. His mother was not sick or poor, but after her husband was injured in a serious accident, she had decided that leaving her boys was somehow the best choice. With a tear-stained face he ran, chasing behind her four wheels as they traveled out of sight, stealing the only life he had ever known out from under him. He would never let go of the moment that took his happiness and he would never forget.

I sat in front of him fifty-one years later as he came to terms with the fact that he was dying. Cancer had come knocking, and his body could no longer avoid the call from what would soon be the end. He had walked out on us again a year before, but there we sat in his mother's home. As much as I thought I hated this man, I was at his door as soon as I found out he was sick. We sat in a bright living room, decorated with floral chairs and faint yellow walls. Most would have found the room uplifting, but as I sat there and looked at the shadow of the man he once was, the heaviness of the room took my breath away. Without fear he said, "Karri, I am dying. It is what I have wanted my whole life. I just want to go home." I realize now that home is what he had really been searching for all those years, and that he ran from his happiness with the same determination that he had when he ran after his mother so many years before. He was that same little boy who just wanted to go home. I saw him with unconditional love in my heart for perhaps the first time in my life. I released all of the pain and resentment that I harbored for him, and I just loved my daddy that day. It was a moment that I will never forget. At nineteen years of age, I realized my daddy packed his suitcase, much like I had, and he managed to make it past that half mile. He kept running where I couldn't. But in the end, he and I both realized that you can never outrun yourself.

I made a promise to myself that day. I swore that I would not let my past dictate my future. I was going to be happy, or die trying. There was no other choice. I would not allow misery or hate to live in my heart for one more minute, and I set out to find my own happiness.

There were times when I failed miserably, and I had to get up every time life knocked me down. Like a lot of people, I realize that choosing happiness is the first step and not giving up is the rest of it. I loved the wrong people, made stupid mistakes, and laughed through the tears often, but I never gave up. I didn't stop trying no matter how many curve balls were thrown my direction.

I know that there are so many who have less than perfect beginnings, and I don't usually talk about mine. I am sharing this now because I want you to understand that what I have written in this book has been written because I want you to find your happiness. I want you see the beauty in this world, and all the magic that having an open heart and loving yourself can bring into your life. I don't want you to spend one moment running down a dirt road towards something you need to let go of, or running away from your own happiness because you think it is too hard. Happiness is always a choice, and sometimes you might find yourself fighting through tears or pain to try for one more day to get where you want to be.

Everyone has experiences that create their beliefs about life and who they are, and everyone has the choice to not accept them if they stand in the way of their goals or finding purpose in life. You will have moments that you can either allow to define you, or use to make you a better and stronger version of the person you are today. You will have experiences that will tear you down, just so that you can build yourself back up. If you want happiness you cannot sit on the sideline of your own life. You must get into the game and play as if your life depends on it. There is no other option that will lead you to the happiness you want, or give you more than what you have today. People may leave you, they may disappoint you, but do not quit. Make decisions that will lead you to a better place, and take a stand for who you are. I promise that it will be worth it.

Section One: Find Your Happiness

Happiness is when what you think, what you say, and what you do are in

harmony.

-Gandhi

THE HAPPINESS SURVEY

When I was growing up, I spent a significant amount of time at my grandma's house. I spent my time climbing trees with the neighbors, putting on my grandmas red lipstick, and watching soap operas, which set me up to develop a flare for sparkle and a little drama. I was probably the only seven-year-old who wanted a bar with crystal glasses in my living room when I grew up—just like Ashley had on *The Young and the Restless*. I walked around in my grandma's big hats, singing and recording interviews on an old cassette recorder. I was going to be a star one day. People would interview me when made it big, and I would tell them all about my life. At the age of ten I developed a love for poetry and started keeping a diary. I wanted to capture every moment and explore my creativity through words and music. If you had asked me then what I would write a book about, my answer would not have been a book like this. It would have been a cross between a Sidney Sheldon novel and an episode of *As the World Turns*.

It wasn't until my forties that I realized what I really wanted to be when I grew up. Through a series of events and choices, I learned that helping others find their joy was what I really wanted to do. As I started working with clients and coaching to personal goal attainment, I realized that most people who struggled with finding happiness also had a hard time defining it. Often my clients found themselves just going with the flow. Life started to happen to them, instead of them creating the lives they wanted. This behavior pushes a person farther away from where they want to be, and ultimately will prevent their happiness. Understand that when you avoid putting in the work that it takes to be an active participant in the creation of the life you want, you start to believe that life is something that happens to you, and this couldn't be further from the truth. Life happens to people who give up, who quit, or who allow the past to dictate their actions today.

Before I started my book I wanted to put some data behind my observations, so I conducted a survey. I surveyed one hundred people who ranged in age from twenty-two to seventy-five, both male and female. I asked them each ten simple questions and was able to validate my observations.

When asked how happy the participants were, 29% answered that they felt their lives were really good. The rest fell within the "my life is okay" to "I am not happy at all" range. Approximately 70% of participants walk around in an "okay" to "not happy at all" existence. This was alarming to me. This would mean that for every ten people you see, about three of them are enjoying their lives. The rest are spending their time feeling okay or worse.

Ironically, money is not as much of an issue as we think. Two percent of people surveyed felt that they did not have enough money. Twelve percent struggled some, however they felt they had enough to make ends meet. Eighty-six percent of people surveyed were comfortable, or felt they had more than enough. When asked to prioritize Money, Comfort, and Happiness, most chose Happiness over the other two, and 0% selected Money.

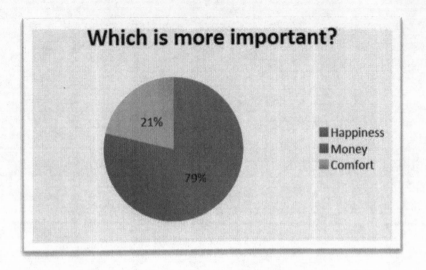

If happiness is the most important thing in life, why are the majority of people not in active pursuit of it? So many lives are spent working to buy houses, cars, vacations, and other material things, but so many are missing the one thing that's most important. If you are not a part of the 29% of happy people today, you have to stop and ask yourself why.

Based on survey results, money was the least important part of life, yet when asked about work/life balance, only a little over half of participants admitted that they have good work life balance. The remaining 40% of participants stated that they struggled to make time for fun or vacations and are working their way through life, missing out on a lot of the things that matter most.

This survey portrays an even greater concern when in further responses, 63% stated that they are not living their dreams and an even more alarming 67% said they either don't know where they want to be in life or have no idea how to get there. My dear friend, we have a problem.

Having a good support system encourages success and provides a key motivator to create happiness. If your relationships cause unwanted stress or conflict, you waste energy fixing connections rather than working on yourself. During the survey, I asked how supported participants felt by their friends and family. One hundred percent of the participants said they had the right people to support them.

Twenty-one percent of these stated that they felt more supported when the people in their lives shared like-minded goals or common belief systems. This finding provides evidence for the need to have a support system in your life that includes people who share common goals. Overall, 93% of participants thought they had the right players on their teams. The quality relationships you have allow you to spend your energy working towards happiness and provide a good support system as you set and work towards the achievement of your goals.

Finally, when surveyed about the area of life participants would like to make better, Happiness & Self Awareness came in first.

What Do I Want to Make Better?

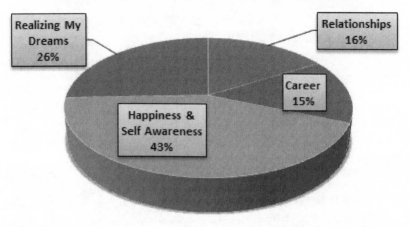

Ultimately, the survey validated my assumption that people want happiness, and struggle with how to get there. This insight has helped me to craft this book with the intention of getting people to a better place in their lives. People are dying to be happy. Everyone wants a greater life experience, yet it's a struggle to get a glimpse of what that means. I hope that as you read this book you stop to reflect on the things that matter most to you, and can devise a strong plan to get from here to where you truly want to be. There is no reason that seven out of every ten people should spend another day just okay with the lives they have.

My job as a life coach is not to act as a therapist, but to help you go from a good life to a great life. I make it clear that it is the responsibility of my client to be accountable to their own plan for success and we work together to build the structure needed to accomplish the goals we set up for them. Each one of you possess the answers on how to obtain your own desires. You know yourself. You know your strengths and your weaknesses better than anyone else. For that reason, it is up to you to put in the work. I cannot make you successful, but I can hold you accountable to your plan for success, and help you get you to your desired result.

Throughout the course of this transition, if you have a good support system, use them. Lean on the people who are there for you and who love you most. Ask them to help you stay accountable as you strive to reach your goals. If you struggle with that support, hire a coach to help you. Everyone hires vocal coaches, fitness coaches, trainers, and people take lessons for everything. Why not have someone there to coach you through the most important part of life? Find your happiness coach. You owe it to yourself to embrace every moment, and to live passionately. Nothing should stand in your way.

DEFINE YOUR HAPPINESS

I love road trips. They are truly one of my favorite ways to explore new places. Most often when I hit the open road—windows down, music playing, and a great pair of sunglasses on—I have a destination in mind. I have preplanned the way I am going, and have made a list of all the things I need. I check the air in my tires, load my truck, and pack a book to listen to in case I get bored. From roadside assistance to Coke Zeros and Cheetos, I am prepared. I head out and never look back. I never get tired of anticipating the next new place I will see and the best route to get there. There is something about driving down a highway and feeling free. I love every minute of it.

Life is the ultimate road trip. You are constantly

moving forward, and often have prepared as much as you can, hoping that if you forgot something, and you will find it just down the road. Like with any road trip, you should be planning with a destination in mind. How will you get to where you want to be, if you aren't even sure where you are heading? In order to find happiness, you have to take the time to define what that means to you. Without that destination, you will spend a lot of time going down roads that may result in dead ends. You know yourself better than anyone and you cannot depend on others to tell you what happiness is for you.

The US Constitution states that each individual is born with the right to life, liberty, and the pursuit of happiness. Happiness is clearly defined as our right, yet so many people have no clue what that really means. In order to chart out a path to your perfect end result, you must identify what that result is first. There are millions of books

31

in this world on what it is and how to find it. Even the
Dahli Lama has written one. They will ask you if you live in
a positive state of wellbeing, if you are more than content,
if you have experienced joy, but the truth is, you can read
all of these books and if you fail to identify the meaning of
this concept for yourself, it will forever be out of reach.

Happiness for me may be very different than
happiness for you. You have to be honest with yourself,
and look inside to see what being happy means for you.
Honesty is perhaps the greatest obstacle at times. It is easy
to tell yourself little lies to make everything better, but
inevitably there are times in life where the truth of a
situation may change the path that you are on forever. You
must embrace that truth, and allow for the sometimes
harsh reality to move you in a better direction. Do not lie
to yourself about what you want in life. There is no good
that comes from this, and it will limit your growth.

You need three things to get you started on your journey to happiness and they are: a definition of what happiness is for you, the courage to take center stage and be the lead character in your own life, and a strong supporting cast. If you can make these things happen, you have taken the first steps down the path toward something greater than what you have today.

In the movie *The Holiday*, Kate Winslet's character meets Arthur and invites him to dinner. They are seated in a busy restaurant at a table with a white linen tablecloth, and she is taken away by the old stories he shares. As the conversation evolves he tells her that in Hollywood, there is always a leading lady, and a best friend. He comments that she is obviously the leading lady, but for some reason has assigned herself to the role of the best friend. Her response to him is, "You are so right, you are supposed to be the leading lady of your own life for God's sake." Since

2006, this has been my mantra. "Everyone deserves the leading role in their own lives." Never play the small role on your own stage. You are the star of this show and your perception will always be your reality. People have both hated me and loved me for this attitude, but the best part of being the leading lady is that you set the stage. The key to making this a reality is to surround yourself with people that love and support you. Set boundaries, and do not allow for unhealthy attachments to people who will bring you down. Unhealthy relationships will exhaust, you and take time away from the people who will be your support.

YOU WILL ALWAYS FIND WHAT
YOU LOOK FOR

My dad used to tell a story that may possibly be my
one of my favorites. There once was a large city
surrounded by a great wall with guards that sat at the city
gate. One morning, a guard was approached by a traveler
who wished to enter the city. The traveler asked the guard
what the people were like in his city and the guard
responded with a question. He asked the traveler what the
people were like in the traveler's last city. Reflecting on his
journey, the traveler responded that the people were
horrible in his last city. They were thieves, liars, swindlers,
and he'd had an awful experience. The guard at the city
gate responded that the man would find the same kind of
people in this city, and the traveler begrudgingly passed

through the gate.

Later that day, a second traveler approached and asked the guard the same question. The guard then presented the same question to the second traveler. Thinking fondly of his travels, the second traveler's response was quite different. The people in the last city were warm and kind. They opened their city and gave freely to those who entered. There was love and peace. When the guard heard the second traveler's response, he smiled and said, "My friend, you will find the same here." The second traveler smiled back, thanked the guard, and passed through the city gate.

One of life's great lessons is this: you will always find what you look for. You are creator of your life and your story. You have the ability to either see the beauty in this life, or be caught up in the pain. It is the choice of every individual that has ever lived, or will live, on this planet.

I'm sure you've heard the phrase "perception is reality" but what does that really mean? Everyone is born into this world and, during the early years, takes on the views and beliefs of their parents and those they come in contact with. Experience gives a person the opportunity to develop their own belief systems and to gain knowledge. Parents pass their energy and perceptions of reality down to their children, and then those children turn into adults, all with different versions of truth and reality, and they're all trying to get along. People tend to gravitate towards others with similar beliefs, or attitudes, or experiences, because it helps to validate the world as they see it. This validation provides safety and protection from the unknown. It makes you feel like you have the answers to most of life's mysteries, and in turn makes you feel you possess control of your fate or destiny. You maintain the illusion that you control your life, right up until something goes awry. Unforeseen illness, the death of a loved one, conflict in the world, all of the above can rock our controlled environment. Everyone will have their boat rocked at some point in their journey. Everyone will experience something that will make them realize that they have no control. The illusion will shatter, and there you will stand, emotionally naked and ready to face the world as it is instead of as you are.

It is then that you must step back and honestly look at the world around you—at the people you love, and the life that you live—and understand how fleeting a moment can be, and how utterly important it is to embrace every second of this beautiful, crazy, chaotic life.

Seeing the beauty in life is a choice that must be realized. In order to have ultimate happiness, you must partner with faith, and hope, or that true joy everyone searches for will always be just beyond your reach.

In order to build a better reality, your perception must be ever changing and evolving. You must expose yourself to content that challenges your current thoughts and beliefs. I enjoy reading, and I listen to books often. I challenge myself by listening to books that, frankly, piss me off at times. I listen to content that pushes my boundaries and allows me to formulate a broader foundation for my own reality. I enjoy reading and listening to books that stimulate my mind, and give perspectives that I had not thought of prior to reading or hearing them.

Broaden your exposure to other cultures, and other people. One of the greatest things I ever did was fly off to Argentina for a year and a half to be submersed in another culture, and to learn the customs and language of that beautiful country. Embrace diversity with respect for others and respect for yourself. Open your mind to the realization that we are all part of a wonderful world with mysteries and moments that are waiting to be discovered.

Look for ways to develop your mind, and do not get tied to having everything look a certain way for the sake of control. Often a person's frustration with life is a direct result of their need to have control over a situation. You are meant to create, not control, your existence. If you can embrace the idea of creating your life, instead of controlling it, you will be closer to having the life you really want.

If you doubt the fact that a person always finds what they look for, I recommend you read the book *E2* by Pam Grout. Each chapter is a new experiment that solidifies the point I am making here. Life does not create you, you create life.

One of my favorite experiments from this book is

one that proves that we find what we look for. Pam tells the reader to pick a color of car, or a color of butterfly, and over a forty-eight-hour period of time, to set the intention to see the color they have selected.

When my nephew and I were coming back from Utah after Christmas last year, I played this audio book as we traveled. He—being the fifteen year old that he is—slept most of the way, but he was awake for this chapter. I paused the audio book and we decided to set an intention together to see yellow cars. During the course of the week that he was with me, we saw yellow cars everywhere.

To give you an idea of how fun and amazing this experiment is, I have to share that I live on a dirt road out in the desert. If a car goes down my road, it is a miracle. We were outside one afternoon during that week, and we saw two yellow cars go down the paved road that intersects with mine. In a random moment while we were outside, two yellow cars passed us when we were basically out in the middle of nowhere, Arizona. If that doesn't give further evidence that we find what we look for, I'm not sure what will.

Why is this important? If the principle that you find what you look for is true, you can either use this to your advantage, or to your detriment. You have to look for your dreams and your vision of the world as you want to experience it, or you will never find it. When you are setting out to create a new life for yourself, you must visualize the desired result. In order to succeed, you must believe that you can achieve your goal and reach the desired destination. That new perception must become your reality. Have faith and hope in the life you want to be living, and begin to live it as if it has already been achieved. Remove words like maybe, hopefully, and probably from your vocabulary, and focus on the fact that you are the person who is living the dream you envision.

Anytime you make a change, you will experience moments of doubt because you are rocking the reality you have believed in, in order to build a new one. There is no space for doubt during this evolution. You are not allowed to doubt the person you are. It is unnecessary, and will provide another obstacle that you will then have to overcome. You are better than that. You deserve more than what that thought process allows. Break those chains and remove the need to control the result. Instead, focus on the freedom to be who you are, and respect the best version of yourself.

GET WHAT YOU WANT

With every job that I have ever had, I have immediately started my pursuit to move up in the company. I am an ambitious person and advancement has always been my choice. I'm sure you can tell by what I have shared so far that sitting still has never been much of an option for me. I am the person who longs to take a nap on a Saturday or Sunday afternoon and then after twenty minutes I get up and get back to doing something. My friends get annoyed when we watch movies because, unless I am at a theater, I am doing something else the entire time. There are days where I decide I want to disconnect and do nothing, which works for about ten minutes and then I find myself in the garage trying to build something.

I have worked very hard to be the best in every job

that I have ever had. I am not saying that I have been the best; I am saying that if I was not successful, it wasn't because I was sitting on a sideline somewhere.

There came a time in my life when I needed a change, and transferring with my company became an option. Looking back at it now, I realize that choosing to transfer was more for me personally than professionally. I had come to a crossroads in my personal life where what I was doing, and the relationship I was in were going nowhere. I needed to cut ties, and move on to a bigger and better adventure for myself. The person who offered me the position told me exactly what I needed to hear to help me make the move. I was going to start in a different position and prove that I was worthy for advancement yet again. Woo-hoo, I was on my way. I sold my house, packed up, and headed to sunny Arizona. I hit that job like a category four hurricane. I did everything that I needed to do to advance and move in the same direction I always do. Then something happened. I ended up in a position with a boss that did not value my contribution. She saw my performance as a threat. She did not value my efforts, and while I was putting in more and more time in the office, it became clear that it would never be enough. I found myself in a place of regret. I questioned my future with the company and, most often, my sanity for making the decision to leave my family and the life I had created, for the cause of moving up and being ambitious. I was working long hours and had no down time. It was a time in my life where I realized something needed to change yet again. The frustration I felt was a barrier for me, and I had to take a long look in the mirror and decide what I really wanted. This woman was everything a manager should never be, and I was not about to give my happiness over to someone who didn't deserve it.

As the days went on, I had to sit down and really assess what I liked to do, and for the first time in my professional career, what I wanted to do. The answer had always been to move up and now it wasn't. There comes a time in your life when what has served you in the past no longer serves your present or future, and that moment is when hard decisions come into play.

I made a list of all the things that I enjoyed about my current role because I knew that if I was going to leave the company, it would be for a job I loved.

I had no idea at the time that this experience, or that list, would lead me to do what I am doing today, but it did. In that moment of honesty and self-discovery, I realized that my favorite job was coaching people. It was helping my employees find their happiness so that they enjoyed their work. It was helping them achieve their goals and have rewarding experiences. I loved people and my goal was always happiness for myself and for those that I associated with. I enrolled in my first life coaching course the following week, and obtained my certification eighteen months later.

Had I not been in a situation that sparked that unhappiness and discomfort, I wouldn't be where I am today. Bless that woman's cold heart for being the person she is, but that experience caused the evolution that has me living my dreams and embracing my passion.

I was not in the position to quit my job and move right into my new career at first, but I did reassess my plan within the company, and I ended up with a fantastic boss who was not only a support to me, but also a friend as I worked towards my new goals. There will be times when you find yourself traveling down a road simply because it's on your map. You may even take a turn and hit a dead end, but there is always a reason for it. You have to be open to the *why* behind the experience, and look for a bigger picture at every turn. A dead end is nothing more than an opportunity to turn yourself around and explore a different route.

Sit down and make a list of all the things you love to do. Ask yourself what you want to be when you grow up. I thought I had a plan, and as I got older I let life get in the way. Instead of pursuing an English degree, I chose business and marketing because of a wonderful company benefit. Getting a higher education was always a priority, and part of the reason I stayed with my company. However, as I worked to progress in my career, I moved a little further away from my vision and passion. When I was able to assess the real Karri and what she wanted, I realized it had nothing to do with business and marketing. My passion had nothing to do with the convenience of a company benefit.

When I set out to coach, and help motivate people, I had no idea that it would help me accomplish the dream of my five-year-old self, who wanted to be an author. I never thought writing would be part of it, but suddenly it became the logical next step. As I have worked with clients in realizing their goals and dreams, my own have come alive. I cannot coach someone to do something that I myself am not willing to do.

Assess your dreams; get back to being who you are. If you want to be a chef, go to culinary school. If you want to open a lawn care business, buy that equipment and get out there to talk to people. Make your list of dreams. I promise that you will achieve them with a good plan and some elbow grease. Anything is possible.

Be dedicated. I love to dream, and I can daydream like the best of them, but a daydream does not make your life happen. If you want to make your dreams happen, you cannot sit idly by waiting for them to appear. Although having a vision and seeing your solution is key to getting started, dedication is the elbow grease that will keep pushing you forward when you have to get past your obstacles. Be stubborn and do not give up.

I want to make something very clear, and perhaps anyone who knows me will laugh at the irony of me writing this next sentence. You must be patient. I am fairly certain my mother just fell out of her chair when she realized her daughter wrote that. Patience is not a virtue this girl has ever possessed. When I want something I go for it, and when I want it, chances are I want it by yesterday. That being said, I have realized that endeavors take time. I did not complete my life coaching program and walk out of the house to see people lined up ready to take on their lives with me as their coach. It takes time to get to where you want to be.

Although the end result will take time, it is the journey that will reward you. While I was in my program, the studies and hours I had to put in for coaching never once felt like work. Each week was a new opportunity to explore and learn more about doing something that I love. This is where you want to be. If you are on the path that makes you happy, work doesn't feel like work, and the journey is a lot like living your dreams.

I have a wonderful friend who, after years of marriage and having two beautiful children, decided to go into real estate. She decided to seize the opportunity to do something for herself. The conversations we have had while chasing our dreams have been enlightening, and so rewarding. Although we are pursuing different dreams, the feelings and experiences we share allow for an ultimate support system, especially in the moments where patience is required.

Find a strong support system for yourself. It doesn't matter if it is your spouse, your best friend from high school, or a family member, but find that friend who will be a good listener, and an honest participant in your journey. You could choose to go at it alone, but having that support will help you stay on track. Not only will the accountability be there, but the unconditional love will keep you sane. I don't know what I would have done without my friend, and her support!

So there you have it. There are four things you need to do today to get going on your new life, and really define how to get what you want! All you need is a little plan, a little dedication, some patience, and great support.

It does not matter how old you are, how long you have been doing what you are doing right now, or how hard it may be. If you will just start in the direction of your dreams, and focus on the journey, there will be no more dead ends.

PROCRASTINATION & PASSION

Chances are, you have seen movie stars walking down the red carpet, or giving an award acceptance speech. You have seen them at the Sundance Festival walking around in ski boots and expensive coats and thought, "Man, they are so lucky." Most people would life swap in a second to experience one day like that. Looking in, it's easy to think their lives are so much better than what you have, and get slightly jealous. On the other side of an actress's arm is that famous quarterback who won the Super Bowl last year. He has great hair and is sporting a ring on his left ring finger. The reaction is the same. "Why are they so damn lucky?"

What if I told you that luck had nothing to do with

it? What if it all boils down to hard work and sacrifice? Some might believe me while others mock the thought. For the most part, these successful people are not lucky outside of the potential skill they were born with. They had to put in the work. While I was skipping French class to go play volleyball with the cutest boy in school, the quarterback was practicing and practicing because his dream was more important than the distraction. The actress was practicing her lines for her audition to that next community theater play, hoping to get the lead role. They had similar obstacles to those that all of us had. Some famous people had worse. They lived in less than desirable conditions, and swore that it would not be how their story ended. They fought the odds repeatedly and never gave up. You could argue that for every successful actress or quarterback there are ten more who tried and failed. You would be right. But the difference is they stopped when others didn't.

You have to find your passion in life. We are all guaranteed obstacles. Obstacles are inevitable, and your passion for that which you pursue must be greater than anything else that comes at you. A lot of people have comfortable lives. It's easy to work for someone else. You have vacation time, personal time, a 401k, and a lunch with two additional breaks every day. It is somewhat safe, and that paycheck pays the bills. But what is your passion?

I always ask clients, family, and friends the same question. If you won the lottery today, what would you wake up and do tomorrow? That is a question that always leads people on a path of discovery. Stop and answer that for yourself.

You may not want to pursue your passion as a way to make money, and that is 100% okay. Not everyone needs to do that. But if there is something that you love to do, you need to bring it back into your life. I love to cook. It is something that my mother taught me to do. She grew up in the South, so you can imagine the wonderful recipes that came out of her kitchen. She was self-taught, and did not want her daughters to grow up unable to cook. I remember being three years old, standing in a chair beside her as she cut onions and potatoes, mixed biscuit dough, made gravy, you name it.

As I got older, I started to explore recipes and cuisine outside of what she taught me. I learned to make different foods from all over the world, and became very good at it. I once had an ex-boyfriend ask me if I would teach his girlfriend to cook. I politely declined, but I am sure you get the picture.

Now, at the end of a long work day, I find that some good music and a good recipe are always welcome stress relievers. I have had many people ask me why I haven't opened a restaurant and my response is always the same. "I am too pretty for a hot kitchen." I laugh it off as fact, but the truth is that although it is a passion of mine, and I enjoy it, it is not a passion that I would ever turn into a career. Any professional chef would mock my technique and shake their head at some of the presentations that come out of my kitchen. I cook for people I love. I like intimate dinner parties, and time around a table with those I care about. That is the part I find most enjoyable.

On the flip side, my other passion has always been people's happiness. I have a strong desire to help people discover themselves, and live the lives they dream about, and think impossible. I told someone not too long ago that helping people and listening to them is something I have done all my life for free, and now people pay me for it. That is what I would do tomorrow morning if I won the lottery today. That is what I have turned into my career. The dinner on the table with loved ones is just an added bonus, and something I share freely.

So hopefully at this point you have discovered what your answer is. If not, I suggest you put this book down for a moment and pull out a pen and paper. Before we move on to the procrastination piece of this chapter, I want you to experience that moment of realization. What is your passion? Make a list of all the things you love to do—the things you do when no one has any expectation of you, and when money is no object. I will wait.

Things I like to do:

1.

2.

3.

4.

5.

Welcome back. For some of you, it may take a little time to rediscover yourself. Remember that life is a journey, and sometimes it takes a little while to get back on the right path for you.

Let's talk a little bit about procrastination. Most people associate procrastination with being lazy, but avoidance has many more layers than that. There is fear of rejection, fear of failure, and of course the potential that what you thought was your passion, really isn't. Only you can answer to which one of these plays a role in your procrastination. You owe it to yourself to honestly determine what is holding you back.

Every successful person out there has experienced failure, rejection, and fear. The difference is that their passion was more important that what they felt in a moment. They had a drive and determination to never give up. They created a muscle memory of not quitting, and pressing against any wall that stood in their way, until it came crumbling down.

There is no set time limit on your dreams. There are countless examples of people who have continued on to be successful later in life. Obviously, if your dream was to play professional sports, win the Olympics, or walk down a runway in Milan, those ships may have sailed, but the specifics of how you exhibit your passions are not important. If it is your passion, you will find a way to do it. The key is work. You have to work for what you want. Anything handed to you is never as treasured as something you have worked for.

Go back to your list of things you love to do. Look

at it closely. Of all the passions you have selected, which are you willing to work for? What item on your list matters most to you? Are you doing that today? You have to determine what it will take to get you to the pursuit of that passion, and decide right now to stop waiting. Are your dreams more important than your comfort?

When you procrastinate, and fail to be proactive in your approach to what needs to be done, you become reactionary. You respond to the things that you have to do, and focus on the things that come at you, instead of going out and making things happen. When you begin to live this way, you inadvertently let go of passion and embrace average. Life turns into a task list instead of an action list. You lose drive and motivation. You become exhausted, and turn to the next escape that will make you feel better. Is that what you want? Do you want to exist, or do you want to live?

You may be asking how you get out of the patterns you have created for yourself. How do you change this? It's very simple. It all comes back to that pen and paper. I am naturally a list person. I make lists for everything. This may not be your go-to behavior, and that is okay, but I'd like you to give it a try. When I need to do something that requires work, I make it a process. This is necessary for success. Consider this process a map to living your passion. You need to sit down with some uninterrupted time, and write all of the things that you need to do to get that passion back into your life. You have to make a list and keep writing until you can't write anymore. Once you have this list, prioritize it. What comes first, second, third? I'm sure you get the picture. To the right of each of these, put a date.

Give yourself deadlines. Remember that these are adjustable if needed, but start with a date that you feel is reasonable, and then pull out your calendar. On your calendar, on each of the dates you've chosen, add the items from your list. Congratulations!! You have a plan of attack. You are no longer reacting. You are creating. Put your list somewhere where you can see it every day. Revisit it regularly, and grade yourself on your performance. Make adjustments where needed, but most importantly, do not quit.

You can share this list with a loved one for extra support and accountability. But my friend, you are now on your way to living a more passionate and fulfilling life. Do not stop. That is the key to success. Keep going!

Section Two: Get Out Of

Your Own Way

You've gotta find a way to get out of your own way, so you can progress in life.

- STEVE CARLTON

Like many Southern women, I do love adversity. Looking back, I'm sure that is why I've had some of the relationships I have had in my life. There will be more on that in my second book, coming next spring. I'm thinking of using the title: "You Can't Save Crazy" That should give you some ideas about what is to come. Anyhow, I enjoy a challenge. I look at it as an opportunity to create a better, more meaningful result. Sometimes it takes a demolition and rebuild, but anything is possible. If metaphorically jumping hurdles were a sport, I would have a gold medal or two. In fact, I once orchestrated a training with onsite support for an entire leadership team, just because my director told me it couldn't be done. After the trainer's travel was booked and the classes were scheduled, I pranced into the director's office and sat down to chat. The conversation started with, "So guess what I did…" It was a good day. Though it wasn't as important to him as it was to me, the satisfaction of doing something that "couldn't be done" was irreplaceable. But what happens when you are the one telling yourself something can't be done? What about when you let perceived obstacles stop you from even attempting to achieve something?

I believe that you can do anything you desire to. You have the power to take your dreams and turn them into a reality, yet in the race of your own life, it's so easy to run towards that first hurdle and stop. Better yet, sometimes there is no hurdle to start with, but that's scary so you move one right onto your track. Imagine watching that event in the Olympics.

Occasionally the hurdles do come from outside sources. Situations in life, and influences of those around you, can create additional obstacles that at times seem insurmountable. Regardless of the source of your obstacles, you must be strong enough to remove them, and believe that you can accomplish anything you put your mind to. Do not let fear or self-doubt stand in the way of what you really want. You may have failures or setbacks, but there are immeasurable opportunities in failure and in weakness. People tend to dream often, and live with those dreams unrealized because procrastination steps in. Procrastination can cause you to lose an opportunity forever, because you just don't do what you need to do.

Growing up on Hilton Head Island, I had the opportunity to attend the Family Circle Cup every year. My dad always brought tickets home to us. Between that and the Heritage Classic golf tournament, I had the opportunity to meet amazing athletes. While in high school, and working at the smallest movie theater on the island, I got to serve popcorn to Mohammad Ali, Billie Jean King, and a few others. I checked out in front of John Mellencamp at the Winn Dixie one Saturday, back when "Cougar" was still his middle name, and I walked with some of the golf greats. Running around that island taught me a lot about what it takes to win, and I had more than a few examples of greatness at every turn.

Perhaps the most impactful experience for me was during the Family Circle cup when I was fifteen years old. It was 1988 and Steffi Graf was the defending champion. Like every year, my dad brought tickets home for us and I couldn't wait to attend. My older brother worked at the tennis club, watering and repairing the clay courts, and I was his sidekick as often as I could be. The morning of Martina Navratilova's big game, my brother received a call to go into work. During the night someone had written slurs that related to Navratilova's sexual preference in the clay of the main court. Not only had someone vandalized the courts, but without immediate repair, the game would be postponed. My brother and his coworkers stepped in and got the job done, and do you know what Navratilova did? She stepped on that newly repaired court and she won that tournament! She took home the championship that year. In the face of adversity, she did not let that obstacle get in her way.

I cannot tell you enough that if you want a better life than what you have today, you need to be the champion it requires. You can quit. You can walk off that court and let life and the actions of others defeat you, or you can jump those hurdles and win the tournament.

A beautiful part of this life is that you do have the ability to achieve greatness. No one can stop you unless you let them. Do not put obstacles in your own way. Move them, and move forward, believing in you, and the power of creation you possess.

I spent a lot of years in my own dark ages working through obstacles, and my love of adversity and winning made me push forward through them. I have struggled to achieve goals and I have experienced setbacks, but the greatest aha moment for me was when I started to understand that I had to want success more than the obstacles wanted to stand in my way. Procrastination and passion do not live in the same moment. When you truly want something, and combine that desire with the belief that you can have it, passion will surpass everything else. If that is not how you feel about your current pursuits, it's time to reassess the *why* behind the desire. It's important to discuss what you need to do in this situation, but first it's important to know what not to do.

GIVING UP WHAT YOU WANT FOR COMFORT

One of the hardest obstacles for people to overcome is not what you would assume. We talk about valid obstacles like fear, self-sabotage, and lack of ambition, when in reality, the biggest obstacle for most of us is giving up the comfort of what we know, to embrace a new world that we do not.

Making a change to get to a better place most often requires that you shut down the reactionary cycles that so many find themselves in, and trade them for a proactive approach. Often in life, people react to their circumstances. If I am hungry I make food. If I have work at a certain time, I get up and get there. Most every day there is some scenario that you will find this to be true. People scan

Pinterest for quotes, scroll through Instagram for motivation, and use Facebook as a comparative for their own narratives, but ultimately are defeated before they even begin to act because they lack the ability to risk what they have today for a much better tomorrow.

As human beings, we strive for comfort. It is imbedded in our DNA. We build communities and support systems to remove challenges and provide safety. We use technology and innovation to make our lives easier, and to work smart over working hard. Often we like to play it safe to preserve that comfort. Then we go out and drive fast cars, gamble, jump out of airplanes, and ride roller coasters to get that high that we need, but work so hard to remove. It is so easy to find yourself working jobs you don't love, staying in relationships that hurt you, and replacing your dreams for the nine-to-five with weekends off, vacation time, and 401k existence. If this is not your dream life, there is a part of you that will be left unfulfilled and bored. This is not living, it is mere existence, and no one was born to merely exist.

I have worked in the corporate environment and in leadership roles most of my adult life. I enjoy the energy, the deadlines, the goals, and the impact to the bottom line. I have had the opportunity to coach many direct reports, and it's not hard to see when someone is unfulfilled in life, even though they are comfortable in their career.

I once had an employee who performed well in his role, and had worked in the company for just over a year. I will call him John. John showed up on time to work, he executed his priorities well, and he never complained. During one of our weekly meetings I realized that he was pushing through our conversations in order to get by, but would not actually engage with me, nor the rest of the team. He was quiet, and seemed bored. One day, after a team meeting, I pulled John over to my desk to chat. During the course of the conversation I asked him some challenging questions, and his answers made it clear that this job was not his dream job. He was bored and unhappy. He was going to school to be a welder, and had taken this job to play it safe. The corporate environment always seems like a safe route. Although John was playing it "safe" he was miserable. He admitted to me that he would arrive at work early and sit in the parking lot dreading the fact that he would have to come into the building. At lunch, he would go back to his car to escape the atmosphere, and at the end of the day he would run and never look back.

Concerned for him, and ultimately his happiness, I pushed him to see what he really wanted. Within a matter of weeks, he had decided to pursue his dreams, and had submitted his two weeks' notice with the company. When we sat down to talk during his last week in the office, he thanked me for helping him see where he really wanted to be, and realize the changes he had to make. Sometimes it takes another set of eyes to do so, but when you uncover the realization that there is a better life waiting for you, you have two choices. You can continue lying to yourself, or you can do what it takes to make a change. The beauty is that you have the freedom to choose. When you choose to live your dreams, you are as free as you will ever be. In contrast, when you enslave yourself in comfort you will find—as John found—that you feel chained to a life that you really don't want.

I walked him to the door on his last day. I watched him transform from someone so miserable that he wouldn't engage with other human beings, to the man who stood before me wearing the biggest smile I have ever seen on his face. As I stood behind a glass window, I watched him drive out of the parking lot and down the road toward the new, much better life that was waiting for him.

If you are not doing what you love today, stop what you're doing. Take a long hard look at your life and ask yourself the difficult questions you have been avoiding. Understand that discomfort leads to growth. Growth leads you to a better life every time. John took a chance on himself and his happiness. He made the choice. Everyone has that choice.

What if John had lied to himself and continued to show up every day and sit in his car dreading that long walk into a job that he couldn't stand? What price do you pay to stay comfortable?

1.   **You do not grow.** When you are reacting to, and not in active pursuit of life, you do not grow. There is

no stimulation for your mind or heart. You go through the motions of life and become somewhat detached. With that detachment, there is an avoidance of evolution.

2. You resent your unrealized dreams. Resentment of the life you were "dealt" replaces the joy of accomplishing your dreams. You will resolve to a belief that you had no choice because it will be easier than dealing with the truth. You have the right to choose between the life you love and the life you just live. But in the end you will resent living over loving every time.

3. You lose opportunities. When you fail to chase your dreams, you miss out on beautiful moments of opportunity. Being on the right path brings

synchronicity into your life. You will put energy into

what you love most, and make it happen. This does not

evolve naturally when you live in avoidance. You will

feel that you are pushing against the tide instead of

moving and flowing with it. Opportunities will escape

you.

4. Your communication breaks down.

Communication is the key in any relationship, and that

includes the one you have with yourself. Your heart and

mind need to communicate with each other. Often this

communication is broken when you are not living your

dreams. Your mind will take over and you will lose

passion. There has to be a unity of mind, body, and

spirit, in order to balance and live a life of harmony. Listen to your heart as much as you listen to your mind, and you will be led down the path that will bring you the most joy.

If you relate to John's experience a little more than you should, take a few minutes and answer these questions for yourself:

1. How happy am I today?

2. How passionate am I about my life?

3. Do I feel like I am missing out on something?

4. What does a perfect day look like for me?

5. What does my day look like today?

6. Do I feel resentment or fear in my current (job, relationship, living situation)?

7. How easy is it to get out of bed in the morning and start my day?

8. Do I often think about vacation time, personal time, or sick time that I can use?

9. How fulfilled am I?

10. What would I do if I won the lottery tomorrow?

If you have opened your eyes and found yourself in a place that you no longer want to be, take a step back and be honest with yourself. Decide today to embrace the life you want and start asking yourself what it will take to get there.

I have had this discussion many times. If I won the lottery tomorrow, I would wake up and meet with people to help them find their happiness. I would write books for a living and travel the world while facilitating seminars to help people explore their dreams, and set up plans to live them. I JUST WON THE LOTTERY, MY FRIEND!

There is no reason that you cannot win the metaphorical lottery in your own life. Sometimes these changes take time. They take planning and effort. But guess what you don't need standing in your way? COMFORT.

One of my favorite places to be is up in Provo Canyon. We used to go frequently to Sundance when I lived there. As you travel up the canyon, there is a beautiful river to your right. I always enjoyed looking at the majestic mountains, but this river was hypnotic to me every time. The rushing cold water flowing powerfully down the mountain was breathtaking. Crashing against the banks with such force, and traveling so fearlessly, it was one of the most captivating scenes to take in. Living your life with passion and power makes it as majestic as that powerful and fierce body of water. In contrast, a body of water that does not flow is putrid and stagnant, and so is a life without passion. Do not sit in that pool of stagnant water one more day.

Break free and be fierce. Live with power, and captivate yourself, and all those who come in contact with you. You will live the life you were born to live when you embrace the life you want.

There is no comfort in the pursuit of your dreams, but you will find more happiness than you ever imagined.

THINGS I BUY MAKE ME HAPPY

I love shopping online for a good deal. I have never been one of those shop 'til you drop girls, but we live in a world where it is convenient to spend money. When you are looking for happiness, there are times when immediate gratification can give you that next little fix or high. It is easy to want things that make you happy and for some, it means drugs or alcohol, for others it could mean QVC. There are so many pitfalls that potentially lead to addiction. I don't think anyone ever starts down that path thinking, "Addiction, here I come," yet, there are countless rehabilitation centers that can verify this is where a lot of people end up.

I once had a friend who was so unhappy with himself that

he didn't want to be sober at all. He was constantly

looking for a way to be just a little checked out. I walked

into his life long after that behavior started, but I was

there for the majority of his recovery process. Being able

to spend that time by his side while he struggled with his

demons gave me insight on how the void of happiness

not only impacts you, but all those who surround you.

I have seen this behavior time and time again. Another

close friend of mine shifted from food to alcohol to drugs

to impulse shopping to try to fill the void. Ruined

relationships and bad credit were iron chains tying her to

a life she didn't want to live anymore. My own father

looked for ways to escape a far from perfect childhood,

and could never overcome his own unhappiness. My

mother worked to pay every debt he incurred trying to

find the next feel good moment.

Everyone likes new things. We all enjoy a new car, a new house, or any other new thing. There is nothing wrong with being a consumer. However, if you are shopping, drinking, popping pills, or doing anything else to supplement a void of happiness, it will be fleeting, and will eventually own you.

It is important to look at your life and to determine if this is the slippery slope you have fallen into. Seeing behaviors and being honest with yourself are the keys to turning this around.

Growing up on Hilton Head Island, I was surrounded by money. Not only did the tourists that visited have a lot of it, but the majority of the people that lived there had even more. My high school parking lot was filled with Mercedes, BMW, and Audi emblems. It was hard to walk two feet without seeing name brands and misery. The haves were greater than the have-nots as in any social class situation, and everyone wanted to be at the top of the food chain. But something interesting happened in this school. The most popular boys were the two children of wonderful musicians, who lived in a modest home, with parents who taught them what happiness really meant. They learned that music was their joy and anyone who knew them saw their passion for it. So imagine, if you will, a lot of kids with a lot of money walking around wanting to be like the boys who came from a home of love and happiness.

This does not mean that it is time to donate all of your possessions and live as a beggar. I am a person who believes in earning money and being proud of your contribution to society. I also really enjoy some good thrift shopping for furniture to refurbish. I am saying you should look at your life right now and determine if the things that you fill your life with are buffers to help you feel better. If you are living in a world where these things are the means to an escape, I really want you to find your way out of this pattern and look for more fulfilling things.

In order to find real happiness, you have to stop filling the emptiness with things that don't matter. In difficult times when I have looked for words of comfort, my mantra has always been that no one can take from you the things that are truly worth having.

When you use material things to bring happiness, understand that the happiness is temporary. New things lose their shine and become old things. The more you finance, the more your things own you and you become tied to them as you work to pay for things that you may not have really needed in the first place. Understand that keeping up with others never got anyone any happiness. Life is not a contest of who can accumulate the most stuff. When you are about to buy something new, ask yourself if you need it first. Equate the purchase to how many hours you will have to work to pay for it. It is a simple way to put any purchase in perspective. Determine the best approach. Take a deep breath and understand that a big sale does not equal an emergency. If you need these things, they will always be there for you to purchase. Remember that balance is always the best approach. I am not telling you to hide your money under your mattress and go without. Instead, I am saying to look for joy outside of consumerism.

Do something that costs nothing. Take a walk, go for a bike ride, go on a hike, or explore a place you have never been. There was a time not too long ago where every Saturday was a new adventure for me. Most often I would go alone but I would find a place to explore and get in my truck and go. I had some of the greatest adventures, and met people that I never would have met otherwise.

Get involved in your community. One of the best things I ever did was volunteer my time in a retirement home. When I was a teenager, my church group would go to this little place on the island and sit with older people. We read to them, and talked with them. I learned to love their stories at a very young age. Hearing about their world and experiences brought joy and taught me more about the need for us to all love each other than any other activity could have. Later, when in Argentina, I had the opportunity to go to an orphanage and play with the most beautiful children I had ever seen. The first time I walked in to see them, I was bombarded by these beautiful souls that needed love. The tears rolled down my face from the moment I walked in and didn't stop until I left. We played games and held babies that the world had forgotten. It was an experience that forever changed my life. Look for these beautiful moments. Share the love that you have inside of you and give it freely. It will make you a better person every time you seek to make someone's day better.

Some of the happiest moments in my life were spent camping with my friends and family. Sitting around a campfire, talking and telling scary stories, were some of the highlights of my life. I look back on the times I spent with my brother, who has since passed, and the most wonderful moments with him were spent talking, baking cookies, and camping. There was a time while on a family trip to Lake Powell that he and I sat together eating cookies and people watching. We laughed until we cried and remembered some of the wonderful times growing up when we thought life was hard. These moments are the moments that bring happiness.

Rebuild the relationships that mean the most to you. Spend time with those people that make positive contributions to your life. Take a walk with them, or invite them into your home to have a meal and sit together. This Southern tradition is a welcome change of pace for many people. Don't rush to the next thing after dinner. Sit and talk with your village. Love each other and find joy in those relationships.

Donate old things. As much as I love to go on treasure hunts, especially for furniture to refurbish, I love cleaning out and getting rid of things I don't need anymore. It feels good to create space. Donating these things to places like the Goodwill, or Salvation Army not only frees your living area of unneeded clutter, but it is a contribution to the community.

If you want to shop, shop. I know that there are a lot of people out there who enjoy the art of shopping. Do it. You have every right to pursue any hobby you chose. But, choose wisely. Know the difference between hobby and solution.

Understand that bills equal stress and too many of these little pieces of paper can tie you to a job, a life, or a routine that leads to unhappiness. Do not spend more than you make, and do not let your material things own you.

Remember that you are loved, and you are enough without new clothes, the next best makeup, or the deal of the moment on QVC. You deserve riches in your life that cannot be taken from you. Search out those wonderful things and build a life that you have always dreamed of.

You are the creator of your own story. More than anything that gives you joy for a moment, look to add things that create long-lasting peace and happiness. Take the steps you need to take to get there. Allow yourself time to evolve, and love the person that you are, more than you love the tangible things that surround you. Share yourself with the world and help make it a better place.

Everyone Should Like Me

When I was eight years old, my dad asked me to take a box of tickets to a teacher at my elementary school for a fundraiser they had been working on. I put them in my backpack, and boarded the bus to New Market Elementary in a very rural part of North Carolina.

As I sat down on the bus, I opened my backpack and started looking at the tickets. They were red with black letters. The boy in the seat in front of me turned around and said, "What's that?" With an air of importance I responded, "My daddy asked me to take them to school." I felt very special. I was a girl with a mission. The little boy looked at me and said, "Can I have one?" I pondered the question for about two seconds, right up until he whined,

"Pleeeaase?" In that moment I knew that giving him one, just one, would make him happy, and he would like me. "Sure." I responded. "But don't tell anyone." He was so happy. He smiled and rushed out a thanks before turning around to look at what he had just acquired. The boy next to him was interested in his friend's new thing and he turned around and asked for one too. I knew I shouldn't give it to him, but his buddy in the seat beside him had one. I couldn't say no. Before long, all the kids around me had one, and they liked me. When I got to school, I was a little nervous. There were ten missing from the box. "No one will notice." I thought to myself and went about my day.

At lunch, more kids came up to me asking for tickets. I was caught up in the moment. These tickets were joy and I was making it rain. They loved me. I was in the spotlight and everyone was winning. I guess you could say I had the Oprah experience. I was eight years old, standing on the lunchroom table yelling, "YOU GET A TICKET, AND YOU GET A TICKET!" This vision in my head stopped abruptly, as the teacher picking the tickets up from me approached. Suddenly everything moved in slow motion. I looked at the teacher as he looked down at me, and I slowly handed him half a box of tickets. All the kids went different directions and there I was alone, facing the consequences. The teacher smiled and said, "Thanks Karri. Where are the rest of the tickets?" Without a second thought I answered, "That's all my dad gave me." He thanked me and mentioned he would give my dad a call as he walked away.

As I sat down at the table, I realized the severity of my actions. My dad was going to kill me. Not only did I give the tickets away, but I just lied. Where were all my new friends now? They had already moved to the next new thing. As I walked out of the lunchroom, I saw one of my beloved tickets on the floor. I picked it up and put it in my pocket.

Dreading what would happen after school, I prayed for time to stop. Going home was not what I wanted to do at three o'clock. When the time came, I boarded the same bus that had made me a star that morning and not one kid asked for my autograph. My fame had come to an end. They liked me for a minute because of what I could give them, and now all my fans were gone. I was left to face the music and that music was a dad, who seemed to me like a giant, and he was gonna be pissed.

I got off the bus and went into the house. My dad was in the living room on the couch waiting for me. He asked me to sit down and as I sat as far from him as I could, he said that the teacher called him about some missing tickets. I immediately started to cry. He asked me what was wrong,

Karri J. McClure

and I sang like a bird. I told him what I had done, and that I had done it all for fame. In that moment there was no punishment he could have given me that would have been more effective than the guilt I felt. He must have taken pity on his little girl in that moment because there was no anger. He began to explain to me why those tickets were important. They were charity tickets to be sold for an event that would benefit the school sports program, and he had trusted me with the task of delivering them. He then asked me if I thought the kids I gave them to appreciate how important those tickets were. I thought back to the one I found on the lunchroom floor that was still in my pocket and said no.

He then said something to me that has stuck with me forever. He said, "Karri, people will always like what others can do for them, but the people worth having around you are the ones that like you for you, and not for what they can take from you."

I am not sure I understood that at eight years old, as much as I grew to understand it in my thirties. I always wanted to see people happy, and often became encircled in relationships where I gave and got nothing in return. There were times in my life where I had a lot of people that liked me, but I felt empty.

I had to learn, through a few very tough experiences, that not everyone will like you. Some people are okay with that, and some are not. We cannot be everything to everyone and still be there for ourselves. Love is not about taking, it is about giving, however if you are the one giving all the time, you have to look at the relationship and ask how it helps you to be a happier person.

I know that some relationships are easier to move on from than others. Maybe it isn't about breaking off the relationship in every instance. Instead, perhaps it is about setting the right boundaries with people, and evolving your relationships into much more fulfilling ones.

If you are in a relationship today that is exhausting, or that hurts you more than it makes you happy, ask yourself why. For me, this was a difficult thing to do, and it took time to evolve. Do not beat yourself up, and try to understand that having the proper boundaries will give you more. It is okay to want more out of life, and more out of the people with whom you share your life.

Looking back at the ticket scandal that I survived in 1981, I realize the hardship my actions had on my dad. They had to remake all of the tickets because I had given them away. It took time and money. I did not have any better friends than I had before that incident. I learned that my daddy loved me enough to help me with the lesson, instead of punishing me for my actions, and at the end of it all, he helped set a foundation I could come back to when I struggled with harder lessons down the road.

In my mid-thirties I had circled through so many relationships that had "taken" from me. I remember looking in the mirror one morning as I got ready for work. I realized that I did not recognize myself anymore. The woman staring back at me had lost something along the way. I forgot that liking me first was the most important thing. As tears welled in my eyes, I remembered the story that I just shared with all of you and I set out on a path to start liking *me* again. I needed to remember who I was and redefine what made me happy.

I know that everyone has trying moments like that. Do not avoid them. Let me repeat that, DO NOT AVOID THEM. They are the moments in which we grow.

Sometimes these steps are painful, but not nearly as painful as avoiding them.

To continue my story, that same year I became my own best friend. I ended a relationship with someone I couldn't give to anymore, and started a new one with myself. I remembered that I love old bookstores and coffee shops. A nice drive in the mountains, on a Saturday morning in July makes me happy. I taught myself to make Thai and Cuban food, while listening to new music with all the windows open and the fresh air blowing through the house. I bought my favorite ice cream, and ate it with my favorite wine. I learned that if you like yourself, when you look in the mirror your best friend smiles back. More important than that, I realized that when you love who you are you do not need validation from anyone else in this world. You do not need to give your tickets away to be loved. The right people show up to love you every time, and none of the other stuff really matters.

Please understand that you do not need to learn to cook Cuban food, or drink wine with ice cream to find that happiness. Create your own path, and most importantly, get to know you. Charles Bukowski said it best in the book *Post Office* when he asked, "Can you remember who you were, before the world told you who you should be?"

I am a giving person, and it is easy for me to get so involved in giving to others that I forget to give to myself. I always have to take a step back when I get in a little too deep, and remember that giving to me is my first priority.

There is a great song by Mama Kin entitled "To My Table" and I refer back to it when I need to assess boundaries with people. The lyrics are my key to remembering that give and take has to be present in a healthy relationship with anyone.

What you got baby?
Are you willing, are you able?
What you got baby?
What are you bringing to my table?

-Mama Kin

Know You Are Enough

Humans are some of the most wonderful creatures on earth. Women are strong, and bold, and captivating. Men protect and provide. We were created to be the most intelligent animals and we use our minds to create the most wonderful world. We think, we love, we feel, and we laugh. The human mind has limitless abilities, yet most everyone gets stuck in the habit of negative self-talk. It's easy to forget how to be comfortable in your own skin, and you end up telling yourself that you are not pretty enough, smart enough, or strong enough. This will destroy your journey to happiness every time. You are your worst critic, and you are not the only one who suffers for it.

When I was a little girl I heard, "Karri, you look just

like your momma." Everywhere I went. I was her carbon copy. I hated hearing it. I thought my momma was beautiful but all I ever heard her say was how ugly she felt or how she needed to lose weight. When people commented on how I looked just like her, instead of making me feel pretty and proud, it made me feel like I wasn't good enough. How often do we project our insecurities out into the world, and cause damage that we are not able to see?

I do not have children of my own, but I have had the opportunity to be an aunt, both to my siblings' children, and to those of close friends. I am in awe of this ability to create little copies of ourselves that we can have such hope for. Every parent wants their children to have a better life than they had. I see parents work tireless hours to provide that opportunity. These smart little babies not only pick up on how we feel about ourselves, but they use it as a baseline for their own self-worth.

My mother is a beautiful, strong, caring woman who has spent her life loving, and forgiving, and laughing. Her only flaw is that she has failed to see the perfection she embodies. Why is it so hard to love and forgive yourself?

If you are using words like, "If only..." "I can't because..." "I am not enough..." or if you are focused on the imperfections you see in yourself, not only are you damaging yourself, but you are potentially damaging the perception of self among all of those who love you most.

This is one of the hardest things to change, yet it is the most important if you are in search of a better life. In order to visualize yourself living the life that you want, you have to believe that you deserve it. Getting rid of the negative things you say and feel about yourself is non-negotiable.

When I am working with clients to overcome this

behavior, there are a couple of exercises I give them. If you struggle with negative self-talk, if you do nothing else this week, you need to make this exercise priority number one.

First, go to your quiet room and sit down. Take a few deep breaths and prepare yourself to dig deep. I want you to make a list of all the things you don't like about yourself on the left side of a page. You will need to keep the right side blank for the second part of this exercise. Your list can include physical, emotional, or intellectual items. You name it. Chances are you have been an expert at negative self-talk for so many years that this should be easy. Keep writing until you can't write anymore. Use tissues as needed.

When you finish this list, you are going to feel pretty crappy. You have just spent time writing all of the things that you dislike about yourself. You are a beautiful, loving, perfectly imperfect creature, and you have been blinded by the world. When this exercise is over you will see it, I promise.

Now, for each line of the page that you have written something on the left, I want you to write the counter statement on the right.

For example, if you wrote, "my teeth are not white enough" on the left, write something about your smile on the right side of the page. "My smile lights up my face." If you wrote, "I am horrible at math," write, "I am a wonderful writer." That is from my personal list.

This part of the exercise may take you the longest, however it is the most important. You cannot walk away from this exercise until you have completed the right column. So ignore the phone, the doorbell, and any other distraction. Finish it.

Have you completed the right side of the paper? If not, do

it. Come back when you are done. Every item on the left must have a positive statement to the right. Now you are ready for my favorite part of this exercise. Put your pen down and pick up the piece of paper. Fold the paper right down the middle, separating the left and right columns. Rip the page where you folded it, and make this into two separate lists. Take the left side of the paper and destroy it. Burn it, cut it, ball it up, and throw it in the garbage. Take the remaining list and put it somewhere you will see it every day. I usually put things I need to see on my bathroom mirror, or refrigerator door.

One list will not negate years of being your own bully, but it is the first step to reinforcing how wonderful you are. Every time you hear those sweet nothings in your mind about how you don't measure up, revisit this exercise. A positive thought has so much more power than a negative one.

Your perception of yourself becomes your reality. If you are focused on the negative, you will work towards being all of those things. Every thought precedes a step, and every step leads you to where you feel you deserve to be.

I dated a guy once that I really liked. He was kind, and funny, and I enjoyed the conversations we had. He continually told me that he would never be good enough for me, and I disagreed. However, the more he said it, the more I struggled with seeing him any other way. Trying to combat how he felt about himself was exhausting. It felt like he was shouting the left side of his list every time we spent time together, and I was responding with the right. As time passed, all I could see was how difficult it would be to help him realize his positive contribution in my life. The more he shared his failings, the more I believed him. It built a wall in our relationship, and ultimately ended it. I realized after the relationship ended that not only did he feel that he would never measure up, but that was his comfort zone. If he stayed on the left side of the page, he didn't have to try to be better. It was an excuse to be a victim.

From that point on, if a man ever told me that he wasn't good enough, I believed him and moved along quickly. You are who you perceive yourself to be. In order to give up what you have for what you want, you have to see yourself in the life you want. Believing that you can make a difference in your own life is the first step.

Imagine sitting down to a job interview and only sharing the parts of yourself that you like the least. It is a funny thought now, but every time you interact with someone, if you are focused on what you perceive to be your faults, that is what you share with everyone. Your energy is lower, your body language screams it, and everyone you come in contact with responds to it.

It is so important to have confidence in yourself. I once told someone that I am my own best friend first. This is not selfish, it is necessary. You have to be able to give yourself the kind of love you want from others, before you will be accepting of it from any other source.

People who fail to love themselves cannot truly provide love to any other person. Once you break that barrier and stop being your own critic, amazing things start to happen. People will see you in a different light. You will shine with the strengths you have captured on the right side of your page.

I know that this exercise is more difficult than you anticipated. It leverages honesty, and brings up a lot of emotion in every client who has done it with me. There is a moment when you have to stop doing what you are doing today, and start doing what will bring you a better tomorrow. You need to develop that ability if you are going to succeed. This is your life and it needs to be the best life possible. You owe it to yourself, and to those who see the beauty you are.

If you struggle with this change, sit down with someone who loves you, and ask them to describe you from their perspective. It will help you to see the contribution you make to their lives. It's time you start treating yourself the way you want to be treated. Open your eyes and see yourself the way that others see you. I guarantee you deserve it.

"Negative Nelly saves the day!" said NO ONE EVER

I am that positive person who makes negative people angry. I always look for the best solution with an overly optimistic approach. Before we get too deep into discussing the differences, and how to be more positive, I want to state the most important sentence of this chapter. **Being positive is a choice.**

There isn't a person in this life that hasn't had a moment when they wanted to sit their ass in the dirt and give up. When giving up seems like a good option you have to take a step back, take a really deep breath, and refuse to give into the defeat of that moment. There are endless opportunities to gain experience in this life, and taking the time to see the blessings in every one of them is a gift. I had a conversation with a dear friend recently, about some of the harder things that happened in our childhoods. I will not give energy to them by sharing them in this chapter, but I will share that during the course of our conversation, we spoke of these obstacles with gratitude for strength. Every opportunity we have to gain experience is a blessing, and it can be beautiful. The biggest barrier you can put in your own way is to focus on a negative experience more than you focus on the lesson. Pain is inevitable, but personal growth will always be the benefit from those experiences that makes you stronger.

Most Southern women do not hold grudges. We do not let any negative interaction impact the pride we take in being as sweet as peach pie with a tall glass of tea. We simply brush it off with a "Bless your heart, you (insert angry words here)." We pat ourselves on the back for being graceful and dignified in any situation. We kill you with kindness when you have done us wrong, because we understand the long term goal of positivity. This is truly a tradition passed down for generations. I handle negative people and situations like my mother and my grandmother did before me. For reference, spend a Saturday watching *Steel Magnolias* or *Fried Green Tomatoes* and you will see exactly what I am talking about.

Negativity is like mud on a white dress. It is ugly and stains everything it touches. Not only do people avoid you like the plague when you focus on the negative, but that negativity feeds an energy that is harmful. When you make the choice to be pessimistic, you decide to live in a space of blame and resentment. You refuse to see the role you have in your own life, and you develop an attitude of self-denial. Not only is this taxing on you, your health, and your relationships, it destroys any chance you have at happiness.

You will never be happy if you cannot be positive. Holding onto negative energy will make you sick, and hold you back, and nobody wants that. You have every right to be in the space in which you choose to exist. Your freedom to make choices is a gift. I do, however, want to share with you what you miss when you sit on the wrong side of the fence.

1. **You lose all power to make a change.** If life happens to you, there is no room to create a better experience. You have every day to build a better existence than what you had the day before. You were born to create and to explore. Do not sit down in the dirt and wait to be kicked. Look up, be strong, and be the person you want to be.

2. **People will avoid you.** On an energetic level, negativity is exhausting to deal with. The fight is too

much, and because that energy is cancerous, people will want to stay away. A negative person is so concerned with what happens to them that they fail to create loving and collaborative relationships with others. You will be so busy worrying about what is happening to you, you won't even think to ask about anyone else.

3. **You will be miserable.** Happiness and negativity cannot dwell in the same space. You will be so focused on the things that go wrong, that you will not feel peace.

4. **You will miss out on forgiveness.** Blame is the opposite of forgiveness, and forgiveness is beautiful. If you choose not to forgive, you will fail to understand that everyone is doing the best they can with the tools they have in that moment.

5. Life's lessons will escape you. You will repeat negative patterns and choke out the flow of positive energy.

Like all things in life, there is good and bad in every scenario, so we must address the benefits of being negative also. First, your social calendar will be wide open. No one wants to spend time with a pessimist. It's a social repellent. Also, you will never have to worry about calls from friends who might need to talk through something they are struggling with, or need to feel better about themselves. Last, you will never have to worry about being asked to be a motivational speaker. Not only does negativity hurt you, it hurts everyone who surrounds you.

In order to get past negativity, and into a more positive space, you have to turn resentment into forgiveness, and replace blame with understanding. If you have read this far into the chapter, and find yourself wanting to make that shift, keep reading. This next part will help you.

Steps to becoming a more positive person:

Step 1: Show gratitude.

First, you must drop your feelings of entitlement and embrace gratitude. This step is very near and dear to my heart. It is so important to be optimistic and to have gratitude in all that you do. If you struggle with finding the qualities for which to be grateful, ask your loved ones which qualities of yours they appreciate most. Start a gratitude journal and make an entry every day. Making this part of your routine will not only help you see the wonderful things you have to be thankful for, but it will shift your energy and you will see a difference in not only your attitude, but how you perceive the world.

Step 2: Surround yourself with positive people.

Every interaction you have is energy transference. You are constantly radiating and absorbing energy, and for this reason you must stay close to positive people. It is difficult to let go of people who bring you negativity, but it is vital to the quality and success of your own life. As you know, two crabs in a bucket will never escape because they will constantly pull each other down. When you are around negative people, your energetic vibration lowers, and you become tired. It is physically exhausting to be in the presence of negativity. You must protect yourself from it.

Step 3: Make Amends.

Forgiveness is perhaps the greatest step you can take. You must forgive everyone who has stood in the way of your happiness at some point. Moving past the interaction to learn the lesson can be difficult at times, but you will learn to appreciate the opportunity to grow each time you do.

Read this next sentence carefully. Not only are you to forgive others, you also need to forgive yourself. Everyone makes mistakes, and in various stages of your life perhaps you were a different person entirely. I look back at my own life, and at some of the decisions I made that were hard to overcome, but that forgiveness was necessary for me to continue to progress and move towards the goals that mattered most. You should never condemn yourself for your past decisions, if you have learned what you needed to learn, and if that experience has brought you to the better version of yourself that you are today.

When I was nine years old, I stole twenty dollars from my grandmother. We stayed at her house often, while my mom worked two jobs to support us. I used to spend a lot of time in her room playing with her makeup and jewelry. I wore her hats and dresses, and brushed my hair at her vanity on a weekly basis. One day while pillaging, I found twenty dollars and took it. I remember sitting on her front porch with the money, trying to decide what to do. My grandmother drank a lot of bourbon, and would never notice that the money was gone. As I sat there on that porch contemplating what I had done, I decided to keep it.

I put it in my pocket, and when I got home I told my mom that I found it outside in the school yard. I kept it for a while, and then finally spent it. I do not remember what I bought with it, but I do remember that I punished myself for that mistake for over ten years. I could never bring myself to tell anyone what I had done, and no matter where we lived or what I did, that memory of the stolen money would haunt me at random times. When my grandmother came to live with my mom years later, I remember going to spend the day with her. I made her lunch and we watched

TV. I gave her a pedicure, and helped her do her hair, and when she went to take a nap I took twenty dollars from my purse and I put it in her wallet. I will never forget the relief I felt for giving her that money back. I am sure that I had spent so much more than that on her multiple times over the years, but it was the symbolism of giving that twenty back to her that finally allowed me to forgive myself. No one cared about the money, and I often wonder if she knew that I took it. It took until I was nineteen years old to get past a bad choice I made when I was nine. You owe it to yourself to forgive the person you were yesterday, and allow the person you are today to grow. Do not stand in your own way. Find a way to make amends and move past it.

There are times when you may harbor feelings towards people who are no longer in your life, and you must figure out a way to get past these feelings to move on. One of the best exercises for this is to write letters to that person, and say all the things you would say if they were sitting right in front of you. Allow yourself the closure you need, in order to move past any issues that need that healing.

Step 4: Avoid Negative Content.

When I finished my Reiki Mastery, I received an attunement. For those of you who are not familiar with this, it is a passing of the Reiki symbols from the teacher to the student, which allows for the practice of energy healing. During this process, your energy and chakras are cleared, and you feel refreshed. In the course, you are told that after the attunement you may be more sensitive to the energy around you. I understood what was said, however I had no clue what I was in for. The following weekend, I decided to watch a movie. The movie I selected was a thriller, like many that I had seen before. As I watched this movie I became anxious. Something didn't feel right to me. I usually enjoyed these movies, but there I sat feeling horrible. I turned the movie off and started a different show, and I realized that it was the energy of the movie that had caused me to feel the things I was feeling. When you watch the news, watch certain movies, or subject yourself to negative content, not only are you continuing the flow of negative energy, you are breeding an environment that is counterproductive to your happiness.

You cannot avoid bad news all the time, but you can strive to balance it with positive stories or inspirational content. This will lift your vibrations, and allow for a more positive day.

I understand that scary movies and thrillers may not impact everyone the way that I was impacted on that particular day, and I am not telling anyone to avoid the movie genre if you love it. I am saying that the next time you are exposed to potentially negative content (sorry reality TV), ask yourself if it has an impact on how you feel, and whether it is helping you achieve your goals.

Energy is all around you, and the evidence that both negative and positive energy have an influence on everything can best be displayed by one of my favorite science experiments.

In 1994 Masaru Emoto proved his theory that positive and negative energy can impact the formation of water crystals when they are exposed to both types through word, music, and prayer. The results proved that prayer, positive words, and music, form beautiful crystals, while words like "evil," "you disgust me," and "you fool," form very different results. For pictures of these experiments, go to: http://www.masaru-emoto.net/english/water-crystal.html. You will be amazed at his findings.

Create positive energy for yourself, and all those with whom you associate. You must turn hostility into friendliness, complaints to gratitude, and self-denial to acceptance, to succeed and to ultimately make your reality the one you have always dreamed of.

Avoid Having Regrets

A couple of years ago, I began working with a client who was looking to make some changes in her personal life. She was successful in her career, and her role as a mother. She and her husband had worked very hard to build a loving environment for her daughter, and she was proud of that, but she felt something was missing. During the course of her sessions we talked through some feelings of resentment that she felt had been standing in the way of her finding complete happiness. During a session of self-discovery, we were able to uncover the true driver of these feelings. It was not resentment, but regret.

Oh sneaky, unavoidable regret. Everyone has been there. After a fight with a loved one, a missed opportunity, or a wrong decision, everyone has felt that rush of emotion and guilt. What if you were able to change your point of view, and instead look at your life as a constant learning opportunity? There would be no regret. In order to have regrets, you have to turn your line of sight to the past, and that means missing your ability to experience the present. There is a way to overcome these trying times, and to move forward with the lessons so you can shift your vision to the present and even the future.

This is what I helped my client do. We addressed the regrets and I asked her how much of her past she could change. The obvious answer was none. Short of building a successful time machine, you have to come to the realization that what has been done is over, and extract the lesson while moving forward.

When I was twenty-one years old, I decided to board a

plane to Argentina. I used the opportunity as a tool to run away from the guilt and regret I felt after my father's death. When he passed away, every fight, every unkind word, and every emotion came flooding through the doors of my soul, and I was ridden with guilt. So obviously, leaving for South America was the best way to handle it. I did not realize at the time that this was what I was doing. I was going to serve, and live there for a year and a half because it was what I was supposed to do. The big picture didn't come for me until much later in my life.

I left Utah four days before Christmas and arrived in Resistencia, Chaco Argentina two days later. The moment of realization for me was when I was boarding the plane in Miami to leave the country and I thought, "What the hell have I committed to?" By then it was too late to turn back.

Upon arriving at the mission office, I was paired with a

girl from Uruguay who spoke no English and I, of course, spoke no Spanish. People around me were conversing in a language that I was sure I had never heard before. We climbed into a taxi that rushed us down old streets with rundown buildings. My companion spoke to the taxi driver as I looked out the window watching barefoot children play, and entire families race down the street on the backs of mopeds. It was hot and the air smelled of dirt and rotten grapefruit. I was alone for the first time in my life. Surrounded by people, and I was utterly alone.

After rushing down street after street, cutting off buses of people and horse drawn carts, with a driver yelling at everyone on the road, we arrived at our new apartment. This building was about twenty feet by twenty feet with one door, one window covered with soap instead of curtains for privacy, and a tin roof. My companion talked to me and I understood nothing. We walked over the threshold to find old bunk beds, a camping stove, a small refrigerator, and a door that led into what I assumed was a bathroom. I stood there in a dress from the Salt Lake City mall, and wondered if I would ever make it out alive. Was this how it ended for me? Alone in a third-world country, looking like a mute because no one understood a word that escaped my lips, I again asked, "What the hell have I done?" The regret I felt for leaving my nice big bedroom, in my nice big house, with my nice-smelling clothes and carpet, was all too strong. It was the first time in my life I had truly felt regret. I knew in my heart that my parents had forgiven every nasty word I had shot their way as a teenager. That was a small regret for my actions, but this nightmare would be a never-ending regret.

My companion's name was Rodriguez. She was a feisty little girl at five foot four, and full of either passion or anger. I still am not sure which. I towered over her, but I said nothing. I sat down on the bottom bunk as she talked to me. The less I understood, the louder she spoke. I nodded my head every once in a while to pretend I got some of it but I didn't. I didn't have a clue. All of a sudden there was a knock at the door. Two guys were there when we opened it. There stood Barlow. He was a couple inches taller than me, and had dark hair and blue eyes. He had come by to check on us and to introduce himself. He was from California and spoke English. He must have seen the relief on my face when I looked at him. I continued to stand there and say nothing as my companion just kept talking and talking and talking. I was beginning to wonder if she ever stopped. Barlow asked me how I was doing and I lied. "I'm great. Just getting used to the language and the taxi drivers," I joked. We all stood there and talked for a while before he mentioned a Christmas party that we were all invited to.

The only thing that I looked forward to on Christmas was being able to call my mom. It was over one-hundred degrees in this God-forsaken country, I was alone, and more than anything, I needed to hear my momma's voice.

Christmas morning arrived and all I could think about was going to one of the Telcom offices to make that phone call to the US. After making an appearance at the weirdest Christmas party I had ever been to, we boarded a bus to go call our families. The bus was full of people and police officers in camouflage with semiautomatic weapons. It was just like anything you would see in the movies with the addition of a very scared white girl who was taller than anyone on the bus.

I walked into the office and entered a room with nothing but an old chair, a shelf, and a telephone on the wall. I entered my calling card and dialed the number. As I waited for the call to go through I thought of Christmas morning with my mom and my brother and sister. It would have been cold with snow on the ground and there would have been a great breakfast, and presents. But there I sat in the heat, sunburned and alone, and covered head to toe in mosquito bites. I was miserable.

My mom answered and I started to cry. I could barely choke out a, "Hey momma." She asked me what was wrong and the flood gates opened. I hated it there. I couldn't understand anything, the people looked at me like I was from another planet, I was tired and hot, and my companion wouldn't stop yelling. After a couple moments of listening, my mom asked me, "Karri, do you want to come home?" I responded, "Yes I do, but I can't. I made a commitment to be here, and there are so many people that are proud of me. I don't want to let them down."

We talked for a while, until the calling card was almost empty. I talked to my brother and sister, and told them that I was okay, and said how much I missed them. As the call came to an end, I felt better. I was given the opportunity to end it all right there. I could have been home in my bed by New Years, but commitment meant more than regret in that moment. That night I devised a plan. I was going to have fun with this adventure. Quitting wasn't an option, so I had to figure out how to make the best of it all and not look back.

It was not easy, but I had to get there. I was going to grow to love it there, or die trying. There was no one in the town who spoke English so that would be my first obstacle. I put away all of my English books, and read in Spanish every day. I carried my dictionary with me like it was a bible, and I looked up every word I didn't recognize. I started to understand my companion first, and I'm not sure if it was because she talked the loudest, or because she talked all the time. She had no compassion for my situation and paid no attention to my trying, which only gave me even more determination.

I started talking to everyone: people on the streets, people in the stores, the neighbors, and the taxi drivers. I didn't care if they could understand me or not. It worked. Within three months I was fluent. People started talking back. I was able to have entire conversations, and there was something amazing happening. I started seeing this world as something different than I had before. The beautiful trees, the kids playing soccer in the dirt, the entire families on the backs of mopeds were all becoming normal to me. I grew to love that country, and when the time came for me to board a plane and return to the United States, I cried more than I ever did on the phone that first Christmas.

I became stronger there, and learned a real lesson about regret. You will never know the path not taken. There is no reason to try to conclude what would have, could have, or should have been. The truth you have is based on the choices you make, and the lives you live. I will never know what would have happened, had I decided to come home early, but I do know that I would have been running from my regrets once again, and I would have missed out on the wonderful adventure that Argentina offered me. I would have never learned the importance of committing to something. I would have never learned to live with dirt floors, or eat cheap produce, or hand wash clothes on a stone tub.

There are two types of regret that you can experience in life. One is regret for actions taken, and the other is for opportunities missed. Neither serves a purpose in the pursuit of happiness. You must release your regrets and move forward, understanding that you can grow from each choice or mistake.

You have the opportunity to start today without them—to live in a world where there is no regretting, only learning. I understand that this is very difficult. You may think your regret anchors you, and gives you moral boundaries as you move towards the next decision in life. But what if it didn't? What if regret actually keeps you from making the next choice that will bring you joy?

You must face regret now, and say goodbye to it. Live your life with intention, and know that every choice leads you to a better version of yourself. Take the time to think through the important choices before you make them. Look at the big picture and keep the things that matter most to you in mind.

My adventure in Argentina started because I wanted

to run from pain instead of facing it. Ironically, in the end I learned who I was and that experience set the foundation for me to be the woman I am today. I lived in a poor country with wonderful people, and I chose to serve those around me. The pain from the beginning was something I needed to face, and I learned to face it with courage.

Section Three: Make it Happen

Once you make a decision, the universe conspires to make it happen.

-Ralph Waldo Emerson

Listen to Your Intuition

You do not need a crystal ball, or some super psychic ability to listen to your gut. You always have natural instincts and intuition to guide you if you will listen. For years man has used this gift to survive, and at one point to even outsmart dinner. Today, when most of the hunting is done at the grocery store and on Amazon, there is a tendency to let go of instinctual activity and rely on external resources. Your instincts become clouded and you lose that muscle memory. You forget to listen to what your mind and heart are telling you, even when listening is what has kept humanity alive and on the right track for generations. The examples of good use of intuition are endless. Everyone knows someone who is still alive because they followed their gut. For me, the realization of how important intuition is came barreling towards me when I lived in Argentina.

I was in a remote area of El Chaco, just outside of Resistencia during their monsoon season. The dirt roads had become mud baths, and in order to walk anywhere we needed rubber boots. I was walking down the street with my companion right after the last storm had passed. The roads were awful and the giant ditches to the sides of them were overflowing with water. We were sliding down a quiet road trying not to fall, and laughing all the way. My companion had decided to cross over a driveway a few yards back, and we were separated by a ditch about four feet deep and three feet wide. I was walking between the road and the ditch when I had the thought, "you should get off the road." I dismissed it, as we were in the middle of a conversation, and the rain was starting to pick up again. We needed to get home before it got worse, and our boots

sticking in the mud every few yards was not helping us at

all.

The thought that I should get off the road passed

through my mind again as a crazy taxi driver made a left

turn and drenched my companion with ditch water. I

thought, "No way. I am staying right here." We made it a

few more feet before I heard a bus behind us. Again I

heard, "you should get off the road," and this time I

listened. I jumped over the ditch and barely landed on the

other side. Within seconds of my landing, the bus that had

been traveling down the road lost control and slid to where

I had just been standing. In shock, I looked at my

companion, and we both realized the catastrophe that I was

able to avoid by seconds. There was no way for us to have

known the bus would lose control, but we did know that

had I been standing in that spot when it happened, my life

most likely would have ended.

So many times I have questioned the difference between my strong-willed determination and my gut intuition. That day however, I knew that it was more than a passing thought. There are countless stories of people listening to their intuition and avoiding tragedy, and I argue that it is also possible to use intuition in our daily lives to make the right decisions, no matter how small.

Intuition isn't always about avoiding dire situations. Last year one of my clients was working to build her business, and scheduling visits to meet with potential clients was obviously a high priority. She found herself slipping because she was struggling to manage all of the administrative tasks, and she felt that this was getting in the way of finding and closing deals with new customers. At her first session, we discussed the hours needed each week to accomplish the tasks on her to do list, and how much time she needed to spend with new customers in order to meet her sales goals. From there we went to work organizing her schedule and prioritizing her tasks. We were able to balance her time and set up a schedule that she would be able to work with. We decided that during our next session we would revisit this strategy and assess how well this was working for her. We would need to determine any adjustments and discuss wins and opportunities for the weeks in between our sessions.

Two weeks later, we met again. She had worked very hard on making new contacts, but had not met her new client goal with the current strategy. We determined that although she'd had the time allotted during the week, something was missing. She explained that she had picked lucrative areas to visit, and had walked into every office without a significant map or approach. She'd found that most of the stores in these areas were very busy, and potential clients were unable to meet with her during the times she had designated in her schedule to make those visits. We'd had a plan but it obviously needed work.

We discussed the thought process for picking the times and locations for these visits. She said that they were logical decisions because she could make the most money in those areas. She was a little frustrated because although the areas were good, the timing was off. I asked her if she was willing to try something different.

I asked her to make a list of all the stores and clients she wanted to visit, and to put a plan together for the following week, but this time I also wanted her to listen to her gut. We agreed that every morning she would review her schedule before leaving her office, and determine whether the schedule she had in place felt right for that day. If it didn't, I asked her to make the changes necessary for it to feel right. She agreed and we set up a follow up call for the next week.

The full week had not passed when I received a call from her. It had only been three days, and she had been so successful with her appointments that she had exceeded her goal for the week and was still going strong. She rescheduled visits that she felt would not be productive. Not only did she schedule her week more proactively, but she also felt her plan would be successful. Her belief that she was on the most productive path led her to the success she was looking for.

Intuition is a powerful thing. I was involved in a relationship a few years back that I tried to force. We were good friends, and had great chemistry. My intuition told me in the beginning not to pursue more than the friendship that I had with this man and I refused to listen. I didn't like the answer so I closed the book and decided to do it all on my own. We became involved, and over time the relationship fell apart. I tried to make it work on multiple occasions, but we became stagnant. Our communication broke down and within a matter of weeks this once close friend was no longer in my life. After moving to Arizona, and taking the time to look at the big picture, I realized that the end was not really a shock at all. He had moved on to a new relationship and we both lost out on a very valuable friendship. Had I listened to my intuition, I am certain that this man would still be in my life.

How do you harness this knowledge in your life to protect, succeed, and love? You know yourself better than anyone else ever could. Be in tune with your instincts. Take some time each day to check in with yourself and assess where you are and what you need to do to make sure you are on the right path for you. Here are some of my

recommendations to help you tune in.

1. **Stop and Listen**. Regardless of how busy you are,

you owe it to yourself to take a few minutes each day to

stop everything. Turn off the radio, TV, and cellphone.

Go to a place where you can be alone for a few minutes,

and take a few deep breaths. Think about what you

want to accomplish and what you need guidance on.

2. **Question and Answer**. This is the key to listening

to your heart. I have a ton of cheap notebooks that I

keep around my house and in my office for exercises

like these. Take out a piece of paper and a pen after you

have removed all of your distractions, and have a

conversation with yourself. What questions can you

pose that will cultivate your truth? An example of a good starter question is, "What is happiness for me?" Then pause for a moment and listen to yourself. Record your questions and answers in your notebook of choice, and keep asking and writing until you can't think of anymore. After you have completed this exercise, read over the questions and answers. If you do this, I promise that you will be surprised at the insight you can gain from the answers your heart has provided you.

3. Determine the approach. Discovering what feels right is the first step; taking action is all of the other steps. Make a plan for how to accomplish the actions that you can pull from your answers. If you use the example question above, after you answer what happiness is for you, explore the answer and look for ways to turn it into a goal while identifying the steps you need to take to get to that end result. These steps and your goal are the beginning of your plan. Mind maps, lists, bubbles, boxes, and arrows are all effective ways to start brainstorming what the approach needs to be. If you struggle with this, set up a session with me, and we will get you going in the right direction.

4. **Test it out.** Congratulations! You have a plan and you have included intuition as a guide. Give yourself a time frame to accomplish these actions and use this plan to have periodic check-ins with yourself. Remember that every day brings a new opportunity to reflect and make your plan better. Be kind to yourself, but hold yourself accountable. If you are not making progress, revisit your plan and ask yourself if this is really what you want.

5. Repeat! The key to winning is never stopping. You must keep moving forward. What people often fail to realize is that if you are not moving forward towards the life you want, you are moving away from it. No one stays in the same place. People are always moving.

You have the ability to hear the promptings of your heart, and to use these messages of love to guide you in the direction of your dreams. I cannot say enough how much you deserve the life that you were born to live. Each one of us has all of the answers we need inside of us. Tapping into those answers is possible and it will take time to learn to listen. It is important to discover how you listen best. Intuition can be used in your personal and professional lives to bring you the success you are looking for.

For those of you who try this five-step method, I would

love to hear back about how it works for you, and hear any

success stories you would like to share. I have provided my

email address at the end of this book, and you can always

contact me on my website: karrijmcclure.com

Know When to Let Go

I have to start this topic off by saying that I am the person you want in your corner. When I really set my sights on a goal, I do not quit. I refuse to walk away, throw in the towel, or concede. That being said, one of the greatest lessons I have had to learn over the last few years is that sometimes you do have to let go. When something you have, or something you are working towards, no longer serves a purpose in the grand scheme of your life, or ultimately hurts you, it is time to let it go. People hold onto comfort and convenience far too often, and it holds them back from a happier and more fulfilling life.

This comes with a caveat. You cannot get discouraged when you realize that you are guilty of this behavior. I'm sure you have dreams and visions of how you want your life to go, and most often reality doesn't measure up. You run late, you get mad, you spill coffee before a big meeting, and you spend way too much time judging your actual life based on the one you envision. This is self-defeating and often leads to unnecessary frustration. Being kind to yourself, and understanding that there will be lessons at the end of every wrong turn, is the key to moving forward. You have to understand that theory and practice are not the same for a reason. It's easy to forget that you are here to make mistakes, and mistakes are where growth occurs.

When I was twenty-six, I went to an open call for plus-sized models. I was so excited. With a professional photographer for a brother, and a sister who did some "regular" modeling in her teens, I had been the thicker sister with a beautiful face. If ONLY I could have been a size two, I could have owned the runways in Milan or so I told myself. Imagine how excited I was when the plus size market took off. I ran into the Hilton Hotel in downtown Salt Lake City, ready to be discovered. This was my time to shine, and that Southern debutante who had never had her party was on like a street light at dusk. This was it. I walked into the ballroom where about 200 other chunky girls awaited their time to shine.

I'm not sure what I expected when I entered, but it wasn't to be sitting in a cattle call with 200 other pretty girls. My confidence wavered as I started to compare myself to everyone else. "Younger than that one, older than her, bigger boobs that her, damn, she forgot her clothes." I was assigned a number to pin to the front of my shirt, and then I took a seat. I went alone, and told no one, to avoid any embarrassing explanation of why it didn't work out— just in case. There I sat, waiting for my number to be

called. Waiting and pushing away thoughts of my
imperfection.

One by one, numbers were called, and girls were
sent through or dismissed. When my time came, I
approached a table with two men, and smiled. I poured on
charm thicker than molasses, and hoped that my looks
would be acceptable. The man on the left asked me to turn
around, and the guy on the right jotted down my responses
to questions that escaped my memory the second it was all
over. Within ten minutes I had been selected, and I
returned to my seat more relieved than excited.

A few minutes passed before all of us who had been
selected were given instructions on how this would all play
out. We would be given the opportunity to go to Seattle
and come face to face with representatives from Lane
Bryant, Vogue, and other print and runway names that I do

not remember now. We would need to provide a portfolio, and plan on two days of meetings, interviews, and classes. That was where the excitement came in. I called my brother as soon as I returned home, and asked that he go with me one Saturday for my photos. I set up vacation time for both jobs, and planned my trip. This was it for me. I was going to live the life I had always wanted, leave my job in sales, and say goodbye to my weekend bar job. I was heading for the big time!

When my time in Seattle came, the realization of having to change my entire life hit me like a ton of bricks, and it was a sacrifice I wasn't willing to make. The only markets for plus size models were in L.A. and New York. It would require money to make money, and it would also require leaving everything behind me. I would have to start my life over, and at twenty-six I was on the tail end for a successful modeling career.

When I returned home, I thought a lot about the sacrifice, and about the forgotten dream that I once had of being a famous movie star so many years before. I was holding onto something that once seemed impossible because I didn't fit the mold. Could I let go of the childhood dream, and create a new opportunity to accept myself just as I was? After consideration, and a boy who asked me not to go, I walked away from it. I realized that my childhood dream wasn't really my passion. I was not willing to turn my entire life upside down for a chance. Dreams change and evolve. It is okay to let go of something that no longer serves your plan. Often when you fight for something, you get so wrapped up in the fight that the actual process becomes more important than the end result. If I had not realized that my unwillingness to give up what I had for something that I wanted meant it wasn't right, I might have made a choice that wasn't the right one for me.

My mom used to say that you won't always know if your decisions are the right ones until you look back at them. You have to make heartfelt decisions for yourself. If you will think through the bigger picture in life and stay in tune with what matters most, you will make the decisions that are best for you in that moment. It doesn't always mean you won't question these choices. After I decided not to go, I continued with school, and started working in the telecommunications industry. The boy who had asked me to stay decided not to take his own advice. Life changed as it always does, and I was thankful that I decided to stay and pursue other dreams. In hindsight, I realized that stardom was not big enough to be my passion, and that my choice was a good one.

Now, when I work with clients, we talk about what

they want. Most of them have dreams they have held onto for years. They have visions of what their lives could be like if they could just get there. Some of them harbor resentment for not achieving these goals. This resentment can lead to regret and block progression. Embrace where you are in the moment, and acknowledge the choices that have led you to where you are right now. Identify what your passion is, and ask yourself this question: is your dream strong enough for you to do whatever it takes to get there? If not, you have to determine what is, and move in that direction. This is where success will be for you. Passion and drive get the job done when dreams and what ifs fail to perform. You have to get behind your decisions and dreams. You have to approach every situation in life with a hell yeah! If your answer is not "hell yeah," then your answer should be "hell no." To that I say, "if the answer is 'hell no' than get the hell out!"

Last year, I had an opportunity to have a relationship with someone who I had known for eleven years. I was interested in someone else when this guy came into my life again. We had been friends and worked together for a long time. I thought I knew him well, and I wanted the Hallmark story placed in my lap. Boy shows up and confesses to girl that he had always had feelings for her. Woo-hoo, It was fate because he said so.

As the relationship got stronger, I suggested a weekend away, and we went. Being with him was like being with a friend that I got to kiss, and I told myself that's how he was so much better than the last guy. Everything was going well until it wasn't. Something just didn't feel right. So I applied the Hell Yeah Rule. It wasn't a HELL YEAH. He was a good guy and we got along well, so I pushed that feeling aside for a couple of weeks to give us more time to "see" if we could have something stronger. The realization came to me again at about three in the morning on a Thursday. I woke up and thought, "This will never be a hell yeah" and I got the hell out. Some people would look at this as a poor decision. I am in my forties after all, and good men are hard to find. For me, it was the only option. I don't need the Hallmark story. I need my story and I need to be constantly moving in the directions of my dreams. If I am going to preach the Hell Yeah Rule, I have to be able to live it. No one wants to live a "maybe" or "let's see what happens" life.

How often have you stayed in a relationship or career where you cannot say "hell yeah" to being there? The experience with this last relationship was the first time that I really took the time to do the right thing, and not stay because I would avoid the conflict by doing so, or because I was close to his kids, or because I knew he would be happier with me than without me. I walked and said "hell yeah" to being single again.

Life is about dreaming and achieving. As I said previously, if you are not moving towards something, you are moving away from it. You never stand still. You have to approach any goal with passion and drive in order to achieve it. The worst mistake you can make is getting into a reactionary routine. If you react to life instead of creating it, you will never have the life that you want or deserve.

Change takes time and you have to be strategic. I am not advising you to go into work tomorrow and say, "This is a hell no, so I'm out." However, if it is a hell no, you have a starting line. Make a plan to make a change. Take some time either alone or with your spouse, and write a description of the life that you want. What do you want to do? What will get you to say, "hell yeah"? Then, figure out how to make that happen.

No one wants to hit the finish line with an okay life.

Live right now, and live with intention. Create the life you

have always dreamed of, and most importantly, know when

to let go.

Embrace Your Detours

The road of life has a lot of twists and turns. This never-ending highway has a lot of exits that lead countless directions. Of course, the quickest way to get from point A to point B is a straight line, and many people logically attempt the most efficient path. Sometimes the exit you are expected to take is missed, and you end up down the road on a detour you anticipated, that you hope will lead you back onto your original road. But most often it takes you onto a brand new one. It is never a straight line for anyone, but imagine all of the scenery you would miss if you never took an exit off of the highway. When I travel, I enjoy taking different streets, and finding places that are never on any tour guide's map. I love discovering new places, and seeing locations that are not in high demand. I enjoy talking to the people, and finding the little local pubs and shops. It is most often what makes my travels the most enjoyable. In life, if you will apply that rule and embrace your detours, there is something wonderful that happens. You have beautiful, unexpected, crazy experiences, and you live. So next time life throws you a detour, use that turn signal and approach it with excitement. You never know what will happen next.

I understand that for some this is a difficult thought process. It used to be for me. I grew up in a very religious family, smack dab in the middle of what they call the "Bible Belt." If you needed a church, you were in the right place. There was one on every corner. There was the Baptist church, the Catholic Church, the Episcopal church, the Lutheran church, the Methodist church, and on, and on, and on. You name it; we all loved Jesus and the twelve. My family didn't belong to any of those churches. We were Mormon. I could write an entire book on how that made for an interesting childhood, and what religious discrimination was like at the age of eight, but this isn't about that.

When you mix Southern skills with Mormon homemaking, you end up skilled in the arts of canning, sewing, cooking, baking, cleaning, and child rearing. I can do most of it quite well. In fact, I am fairly certain I could make a dress out of curtains, can food for a year, and make an old house shine to top the best of them. I was baking cakes, making my own Barbie furniture, and helping take care of my siblings at a very young age.

When I was little, being a writer, a movie star, and a mommy, were all on my to do list. That led to a lot of hilarious and very dramatic tales for the family. I am sure my sister will tell them in her tell-all book one day. I grew up ready to be the best mom and wife in the world. I would go to school, meet Mr. Right (a returned missionary of course), and we would settle in a little town somewhere. I would write books, have some babies, make dinner every night, and we would be happy. Our kids would be close to perfect, and every day would be a fairytale.

As I grew older, I realized this was not really the life I wanted. It is a great story, filled with love and laughter, and it requires some of the best homemaking skills in the world, which I would have been more than capable of, but this was not my story. I know a lot of people who are happy to live this story, and they work hard every day to take care of those babies, and to have dinner on the table every night, however I am too outspoken, too much of a dreamer, and frankly I would have had bourbon hidden around the house just like my grandma did. I would not have been happy.

There was a time in my life where I felt lost. I hadn't quite figured out whether I was living the life I wanted, or the life that I expected. There were many times that I would go to church on Sundays and listen to the talks on family, and the joys of having one, and start to feel guilty. How was I ever going to measure up? The years kept passing month over month, and my Mr. Right never showed up. Luckily, Mr. Wrongs gave me plenty to learn from during that time. I truly went on dates that would make the depression seem like a party. (I will save some of these stories for my next book.)

During my detour, I forgot that life was supposed to be enjoyable. I was so busy trying to hold onto an expectation that even though my new reality was down the road on that next exit, I had stopped my car on the highway of life. I just stayed there with the hazard lights on; not realizing what was ahead of me. Then, I had a moment of clarity. I realized that this is my life, and I get to create it exactly how I want it. Imagine the joy I felt when I realized that the only thing that was keeping me stuck there was the fact that I refused to leave the road I thought I should be on. All I needed to do was make that turn right off the next exit to merge onto the road that was made for me. In that moment, I really started to live. I gained an understanding that I never imagined I would. Life became sweeter to me. The colors were more vivid, the relationships I had with people were stronger, and the guilt I felt was gone.

If you want to be happy, let go of what you expect your life to be, and travel down uncharted roads. There is no adventure, or time for exploration, in expectation. Expectations are the flat tires of this metaphor, my friend. Love every twist and turn on your road, and by all means, stay away from dead ends!

Let go of the fear that stands in your way. Often, people are so afraid of change that they will stay put in the worst scenario for them because it is what they know. Read that again and be honest with yourself. Are you staying in this story because the other story is unknown? Grab that pen and a piece of paper, and write a description of the life you really want. Then start a separate list entitled "Fears." Make a list of the fears that are standing in your way. If you have none, then what are you waiting for? Get out of here, and go live that life. But if you have a list, like the rest of us do, I want you to write why you have that fear beside it. Why do you feel the way you feel? There is a misconception that one's fears will keep them safe. What if I told you that is not always true? In fact, fear and excitement create the same response in your brain. That means that your thoughts make the difference in what you feel, while your body responds in the exact same way for both.

Be excited. I cannot say enough how wonderful it is to realize that you have the ability to create any life you want. Once you have identified your fears, and the reasons behind them, you have to decide that not having the life you want is scarier than the fear of moving past the life you have today. Then, be excited. Embrace the change that is coming your way, and be bold. You are about to be the best version of yourself that you have ever been.

Next, quit trying to be perfect. For a lot of years I avoided things that I didn't think I could be good at. If it did not come easy to me, I didn't do it. It kept me from learning and experiencing growth. We are beautifully imperfect. Start exploring the things that push you to your limits. Do you think Olympians could ski or snowboard the first time they tried? They learned step by step, and they practiced, and failed more times than not. But they did not give up. They pushed themselves and never stopped. I am not telling you to hit the slopes, but I am telling you to get out there and work. Practice and fail over and over again until you get it right. Do not expect to be perfect in this evolution or you will not overcome the obstacles that are before you. Do not quit!

Find a buddy. Change is hard when you go at it alone. This is why people who want to make changes hire life coaches. I remember when I started biking. I had a friend who I started riding with. We rode together about three times a week. It was so much more fun to go with her and her family. I went farther than I ever did alone. We enjoyed talking, and laughing at her kids, as we all rode down the bike paths in Salt Lake. Before too long, we were riding between twelve and eighteen miles a day. We were becoming stronger and getting in better shape, and it was easy because having someone to share it with made it more fun. Go get yourself a buddy to make your change with. Find someone who is supportive, and who understands why you are doing the things you are doing. You need someone to help you address your fears and encourage you to never stop. This is why there are coaches for every sport out there. Why not have a coach for your life? It is much more important than anything else.

Learn to let go of mistakes. This goes hand in hand with not trying to be perfect all the time. When you fail, or hit a road bump, shake it off. I always tell my clients that a speed bump looks so much smaller in your rearview mirror. Imagine if you were in your car, and you came to a speed bump in the road, but instead of going over it and continuing on to your destination, you stopped. There you sit in the road on the speedbump, holding up traffic, not moving. Your errors are the same as those speed bumps. Get over them and keep moving. Get to where you want to go.

The most important part of all of this is to continually visualize where you want to be, and to enjoy yourself while you work to get there. You have an idea of what your life should look like. You know now that you are the creator in this story. Do not lose sight of the end result no matter how hard it feels to get there. Embrace each detour, and know that you are a learning machine. Change requires mistakes and work. You will get there, but the ultimate goal is to enjoy the journey.

I promise that you will succeed if you never give up.

It's Okay to Not Have All the Answers

When I set out to become a life coach, all I had was the vision of what I wanted to do. I really didn't know where to start. My life goal had just made a 180 degree turn.

I sat down and wrote out what I thought my plan should be, and set the intention to make it happen. In came synchronicity. Within a couple of weeks I found the school that I wanted to attend, and enrolled without hesitation. Over the course of the next eighteen months, I completed my courses, and the hours of coaching required for my certification. Everything fell into place and I didn't stop. There were times when keeping my eye on the prize got me through the frustration of a class, or a moment of self-doubt. I knew that in order to live my dream, I could not stop. Quitting was never an option.

When you find that dream that matters more to you than anything else, you don't need all the answers before you start. Most often the answers will change during the process anyway. Do not wait for certainty to make your move. Start down the path to your end result and the answers will come. Treat your new endeavor like a puzzle.

When you open a puzzle, there are pieces that need to be sorted and put together before they create a picture. You have an image of what it's supposed to look like, but you are required to sort piece by piece to make it all fit. It calls for patience and determination. Sometimes the pieces don't fit the way you expect them to, but you adjust and keep trying until it all comes together. Then, if you are like me, you glue it so that you never have to put the damn thing together again.

One of the best ways to visualize your goals and reinforce the path that you have created is to make a vision board. This is an opportunity to put your own puzzle together, and reference it with intention. No life coach worth anything would ever write a book and not talk about a vision board. You have to be able to put your vision together, and this will be a great place to start. Sort through magazines, or search the internet for pictures that represent your goal. Buy some glue, a poster board, and some scissors, and put together a board that will represent where you want to be, and what you want to accomplish. Then, put it somewhere that you will see it every day. This will help you to stay on track and remember that you are working towards something. I make one every January for the coming year. Instead of making resolutions that I will break in a couple of weeks, I map out the things I want to accomplish with pictures, and I keep this map in my closet

to remind myself of what the year will hold for me. I

cannot say this enough; you must be able to see where you

are going if you ever want to get there.

Believe in yourself. You were born to live your life

and actually enjoy it. All of the residual self-doubt no

longer serves you. Do not let it stand in the way of your

dreams. Why waste one more minute not living up to your

potential? You owe it to yourself to dream, and to believe

that you can have anything you want.

There is no reason you will not be able to reach your

goals. Keep them logical, and be mindful of your strengths

as well as your weaknesses. I understand that at some point

we all want to be rock stars, and for most of us that is not a

logical goal. Do not hold onto things that no longer serve

you. When I was in high school, I took private voice

lessons, and this all played into the big movie star dream. I had a beautiful voice, and possibly a real shot at it. I am sure that had I put in the work, I would have accomplished that goal. I look back at the missed opportunity with a greater understanding that as priorities changed, my dreams changed. I loved to sing but I was deathly afraid to do it in front of anyone. Even today, I can stand as a public speaker with no fear or anxiety, however if you asked me to sing, I would probably sit down quickly. I now reserve my singing for the car like everyone else, and I realize that a wish to be a rock star will always be the road not traveled. I have come to terms with it, and removed that obstacle in order to pursue the real things I want to accomplish. Do not let the "coulda, woulda, shoulda" thoughts stand in the way of where you can go today.

Be mindful of past results, or missed opportunities, but do not let the experiences of yesterday hinder your actions today. Failure is part of trying, and there is no need to focus on it. Look at every experience as a possible lesson, and take that lesson with gratitude. Everyone has experiences, but not everyone can stop and see the lesson. Sometimes the lesson is on how to do something again, and sometimes it's on how to avoid that road in the future.

There was a time in my life when I felt that once I hit a certain age, it would all make sense. I thought that on my thirtieth birthday I would wake up, and this life would all make sense. Somehow I would have learned what to do and what not to do, and the mistakes of my past would be my homage to wisdom. I will pause for your laughter so that we can continue. Thirty, thirty-two, thirty-five?? Oh come on. Does this ever end? No, it doesn't. The lessons and experiences will keep on coming. Every day is a new day to learn something. Your thirst and passion should never end. The best part of all of this is that there is no age limit to progression. I don't care what year you were born, you have the right to pursue your dreams. Never let age stand in the way of your goals. You will be wiser tomorrow than you are today, and you have the ability to dream beyond the limits of your current thoughts.

Choose Happiness and Just Say Yes

If you take nothing more away from this book, I want you to have this. Happiness is a choice. At times, that choice is harder to make than others, but it is something you need to strive for if you want something better than what you have today. The concept of there being a better life tomorrow is false. You have to start right now, and say yes to happiness. The path to something better begins with the first step.

If you are not happy today, you will not automatically wake up next Tuesday and proclaim happiness. If you adhere to the belief that the more you suffer in this life, the greater your reward in the next, you should probably stop that. I am pretty sure the message is that men are to have joy. The joy that comes from being true to yourself is immeasurable, and the sooner you can get going with that, the better off you, and everyone who loves you, will be.

In order to find your happiness, you have got to start today. Make the choice right now to be passionate, to be joyful, and to realize that you need to say yes to the life you deserve. Procrastination will keep you from the future you want. Do not put your plan off for one more day. Stop saying that in the future it will be better. Make it better today. Make a goal list, and align each goal with the tasks or actions that you need to complete for each item. Start looking for ways to accomplish what you want. If you are unsure of what you want, start with the things that you like to do. Refer to the question, "If I won the lottery tomorrow, what would I do?"

Take some time to research the things you enjoy, and see what career opportunities might be associated with those things. Hire a life coach to help you organize your plan, and to help hold you accountable. (Ah hummm, I know a really good one.)

When you are looking at the big picture, the ultimate change becomes overwhelming. You can take your plan one piece at a time to make it more manageable. Rome was not built in a day, you know. But it was built one stone at a time.

Here are some simple things that you can do to build yourself up and get closer to happiness if you are struggling with where to go from here.

1. **Love yourself.** Be your biggest fan. If you cannot love the person that you are today, you need to take the

steps that will help you start. One of the biggest mistakes you can make is to look for outside validation over loving yourself. If you need help with self-love, I recommend the book *Remembering Wholeness* by Carol Tuttle. It is perhaps the best place to start.

2.   Stop the complaint and blame game. No one wants to hear that shit. Trust me when I say that you are destroying your energy and the vibration that you share with others when you spend time complaining about things that have gone wrong, or blaming others for things that have happened to you. You have been a willing participant in every experience you have ever had, and that is reason enough to move past them. Embrace the lessons, and move on.

3.   **Stop focusing on how you look over who you are.** I get it. I want to look good for that selfie, too. I love makeup, and I don't leave the house without a little preparation. That being said, if you are more worried about the outside than the inside, you will not be happy for long. Build your character and add dimension to your soul.

4.   **Take care of yourself.** Eat the best way for your body, and get some sleep. Vodka and cigarettes are not a balanced meal. Find the best foods for yourself, and take a walk every once in a while. Movement increases the flow of energy, and you will feel better about anything after a good night's sleep.

5.   Stop being afraid. Be fierce instead of fearful. We will all die once, but most of us never really live. Run to the things that scare you. I have found that they look smaller when you are running towards them, than when you run away from them.

6.   Remember that time is never guaranteed. You do not know how much time you will have in this life. Stop waiting to find out.

7.   Wake up. I love to dream, and as I mentioned earlier I am really good at daydreaming, but action is what will turn those dreams into reality.

8.   Let go of the past. Stop reliving a memory or experience. If you are holding on to the past, your hands are too full to grab your future. Drop it like it's hot.

9.   Stop trying to be perfect. You aren't perfect. You are imperfect, sometimes broken, and you are a beautiful, chaotic soul. Embrace and love every imperfection, physical or otherwise.

10.   Open your mind. Things do not have to be a certain way. Explore the world and embrace the beauty of diversity and culture. You do not have to travel to do this; just challenge yourself with new knowledge every day.

11. Stop being too busy. When you are too busy, you miss out on people and events that really matter. I met my soulmate once, but he was so busy that he didn't see me. Slow down and enjoy the people you have in your life before they are gone.

12. Commit and take action. If you cannot commit to yourself, you will never find happiness. I know that sometimes a cheeseburger sounds better than the pants hanging in the closet waiting to be worn. I have a pair of those jeans in my closet right now. If you want the end result, commit to it, and move forward one step at a time.

13. Stop the negativity. You cannot afford negative energy if you want to achieve your goals. Regardless of the source, walk away from it. Take a stand and refuse

it. Live in a positive space, and you will be happy for it.

14. Focus on your goals and rework them as

necessary. Take the time to make your lists and map

out your plans, and revisit them often. You will need to

adjust and make changes. Do not get tied to making it

all looking a certain way, but stay focused on the result.

15. Learn to let go. Sometimes the things that

worked for you yesterday no longer serve you, and you

need to pack them up and throw them out. Do not limit

your energy or potential by holding onto what no longer

serves you.

Above all else, remember to say yes to yourself, to your

life, to your dreams. Do not say no to opportunities

when they will give you the ability to gain experience and create joy. Not using the word "no" is one of the hardest obstacles for clients to overcome. No keeps you where you are right now. No stops your growth. What if you just said yes to every solid opportunity that came to your door? Where would you be now? Do not shy away from new things out of routine or fear. Just say yes!

Be the Person with a Plan

Everyone has things they want to accomplish. One day I want to (fill in the blank). How does a desire or a dream become an accomplishment? It takes work, and in order to do the work, you need a plan.

I am sure you have heard that a dream becomes a goal after it is written. There is a bit more to it than that. Your dream will not feel like work most of the time, but occasionally the tasks that go with it will. I am passionate about a lot of things in my life, however coaching is my dream. When I am working with a client it does not feel like work, but the marketing, the designing, the writing, and the scheduling sure does. If you want to achieve something great, you have to work for it. Staying in the same spot doing the same thing every day doesn't take the effort that turning your entire life upside down does. It will take dedication. A great person who fails to execute and work is never discovered.

Once you have determined your desired result, be the person with a plan. Your dream is now your project and you want to manage it the way you would manage any project. Start from the goal or intention that you have written down, and work your way back to where you are now. If I want to run a marathon (this will never happen), I have to train myself to run twenty-six miles. No one heads down the block one day, and runs twenty-six miles the next. If the marathon is a year away, I will chart out where I need to be each month so that I can push myself a little bit harder every week to ensure that I get to the goal.

With anything you want to accomplish, you have to

set the goal and set checkpoints for yourself to ensure you stay on track. I do this with everything that I want to accomplish. Even this book started as a list of ideas in an excel spreadsheet. I thought through all of the things I would want to share with a client sitting in front of me, and then put together a plan to get it all on paper. When I set out to write this book, the first thing I did was set up a plan and make deadlines for myself. Sometimes I had to reassess those deadlines, allow for changes, and understand that sometimes I would stick to that plan more than others. But I always had a plan. Just like energy or water, our lives are fluid, and a plan is a tool. Like any tool, it can be improved upon and replaced. I threw away twenty-five pages that I had written according to my plan, because when I read them there was not enough feeling, and I needed to feel this book. An entire day's work was in the garbage, but I never threw away my plan. I just had to recreate it. Here are some tips for you as you work on your plan.

1.   **Keep your eye on the prize.** You have to want it more than you want anything else or it will not be a priority. You may have days where you question the goal. You will have moments when you will want to throw in the towel, but if you are focused, and you really want it, those days will be minor setbacks that you will overcome. If not, you will fail. Before you get started you have to make sure this is really what you want.

2.   **Make your list.** What do you need to do to get where you want to be? Start a list of everything you will potentially need to do. Lists are ever changing and

evolving. Be open to creating a new draft as needed.

The plan to accomplish something is never static.

3.   **Set your priorities.** You have brainstormed, and

you are sitting there staring at your list. Now what? Put

your list in order of importance. What comes first? Can

you assign due dates to each step you have charted out?

If so, do it.

4.   **Be realistic.** When you are setting deadlines for

yourself, you have to be realistic. If I want to lose

twenty pounds, I can't put a deadline at thirty days. I

will fail. You have to really think through the amount of

time and effort that it will take to accomplish each task.

Be flexible, and understand that uncontrollable

situations may pop up that will require reassessment of

your strategy. You still have to maintain your current life and all of your obligations while working towards your goal.

5. **Dedicate time and space to accomplishing your goals.** Where will you accomplish these tasks? Do you need a place to work and focus? I worked with a client once who had small children, and while she was working towards her goal, she was constantly being pulled away, when she needed to work and study. During our sessions, we set up her plan to remove the distraction. She decided that she would go to the library three times every week to work on her tasks. At first, three times a week didn't seem like enough for her, but I asked her to give it a try. We would have a follow up meeting two weeks later and assess the plan to see if it worked. At our next appointment, she shared that

although she wasn't working on her goal every day the way she had originally planned, by dedicating a time and a place, she had worked more efficiently and was producing more of a result in those three times a week than she was when she tried to work every day.

6. **Remove distractions.** We all have distractions and I have more than a few "squirrel!" moments. When I need to focus on my writing, I turn off my phone, lock all the doors, and shut off all music and television. I'd found my phone to be a big distraction while writing, and once I figured out how to manage the distraction, I became more efficient that I ever had been before.

7. **Trust the process.** When you create a plan to accomplish your goals, you set in motion all of the

things that you need to do to get to your finish line. Although you may need to reassess and change the plan, you must always trust the process. Do not doubt your plan.

8.   **Be accountable.** If you are not able to stay on track, ask yourself why. Hold yourself accountable. If your plan isn't working, rebuild and restructure it into something that will work. If you need someone else to hold you accountable, find that person. The majority of my sessions with clients are focused on the accountability. If you cannot be accountable alone, search out that person who will help you succeed. The only reason you will fail is if you stop doing what you need to do to get to your end result.

9.   **Celebrate.** You deserve to enjoy the process. This is your life, and you deserve a party. Build a reward system into your plan. This will help you to stay on track. We all have different motivations, but everyone enjoys a reward. Travel has always been a valuable reward for me. I plan a big trip every year, and I use it to keep me motivated. I spent my birthday this year in Telluride, Colorado exploring and putting the final touches on this book.

10.   **Listen to yourself.** One of the most important principles of life coaching is that each person has the answers inside of them. When I coach a client, I do not develop their plan for them. I help them develop a plan for themselves. If I make a plan for you, it becomes my plan, not yours. You have to create the steps that you need to take, to get to where you want to go. Only then

will you be truly invested in your process. Do not let others tell you what you need to do to get there. Listen to your instinct, your gut, and your heart. This is the only way to be successful.

Remember that you are doing this because this is what matters most to you. Be strong, and don't give up. The joy and satisfaction you will feel once you have accomplished what you set out to do will take your breath away.

Section Four: Be Your Own Best

Friend

"Self-approval and self-acceptance in the now are the main keys to positive changes

in every area of our lives."

-Louise Hay

This section was not part of my original manuscript. In fact, I was working on a workbook section to wrap it all up, and provide some exercises in self-discovery. Then something happened. Over the last few weeks, I have dreamed of memories that tested my love for myself. Life has bombarded me with experiences that have reminded me of the real driver behind any change. As I considered those instances, where I had taken a step back and chosen myself and my love for myself, over situations that were attempting to push me in other directions, the path to wrapping up this book became clear. The workbook will have to wait, because this next part is the most important part.

I have written some of my most heartfelt and life-changing experiences in this book, and as I have read these pages I have grown to feel naked before the metaphoric crowd. This is something that I would have never had the courage to do in years past. But today, being the woman that I have always wanted to be, the desire to share a glimpse of how I found happiness, and grew secure with the woman I have become, has made this possible.

There is no greater goal in life than to achieve self-love: to embrace the woman or man that you are with a reverence and respect for the battle scars life experience has given you. To love your imperfections, and embrace the unique individual that you are, is happiness. You must let go of what society has told you about the person you should be, and walk away from the judgments of others. There will always be hardships, and trials that have the potential to shake you to the core, however you have the power to repel any negative energy that comes your way if you will just remember who you are and the gifts that you bring to this world.

If you cannot believe in yourself, it will stand in the way of your dreams, and nothing will change. You will find yourself in the same place, relationships, and situations, longing for something more than what you have today. Now is the time to stop the cycles that you have lived in, and take a stand for who you are and what you want out of life. Show this life that you are its creator and no one can take that away from you.

Love Who You Are

Growing up in a religious home had a lot of advantages. I learned to believe in a higher power, I gained a sense of community, I learned that selfless service is beautiful for both those who give it, and those who receive it, and I learned that unconditional love is present everywhere if only you believe in it. That being said, there was one misconception that my background gave me, and that was the belief that we are required to be perfect and anything less isn't enough. I'm not sure if it was a combination of my personality and the strong moral compass that was instilled in me at a young age that set me up for a lot of that, but over the course of my life, I have gained a lot of experience in imperfection. I can assure you that we are here to be imperfect. The lesson comes in the mistake more often than not, and the experiences of both our good and bad choices make us the people that we are. You cannot live in a world where you dwell on your imperfections, and love yourself at the same time. Be grateful for all the tears, in moments of joy, and in moments of sadness. Your value is immeasurable and you must stop denying the self-love that you need to withstand the trails that life has to offer. Forgive yourself for making bad choices, and for not living up to the person you thought you should be when you were a kid, and love who you are today.

In my life I have had more than a few instances where I didn't feel like I fit in. Freedom came when I realized that everyone has those. Everyone has moments when they feel like a square peg in a round hole, but the strong ones make a square hole. You are the trailblazer in your own life, and no one can dictate your potential unless you allow it.

I remember arriving in Argentina at the age of twenty-one and realizing that I was about a foot taller than most of the women there. At five foot eight, I was not a giant in the US, but there I felt huge. I was told I was too tall, that had big feet, and the looks on people's faces at times caused a little embarrassment. I have never been dainty, and never will be. It was quite the experience. At first, I shied away from the topic because it made me feel uncomfortable, but as time passed I got used to it, and I would respond that I was the shortest in my family. I would say that if they thought I was huge, they should see the rest of them. The response brought laughter every time, and because I was comfortable with who I was, they were drawn to me as a person, and all was well. I have often wondered what my experience would have been if I had let that situation define me as a person. If I had let insecurity step in, and had become offended when these conversations took place, I would have suffered, and felt like I wasn't enough.

I had to learn at a young age that I was enough, and people would love me just as I was. It took many years of trying to fit into a mold, or a way-too-tight pair of jeans, before I got there, but I finally got there. I had to see my imperfections as a part of me, just like my perfections. Yes, we all have perfections, and the sooner you can identify yours before diving into your imperfections, the happier you will be. Here is a little secret for you: the man or woman who you think has it all, looks in the mirror the same way you do every morning. Stop worrying about what everyone else thinks, or has, and focus more on what you have that makes you the wonderful person that you are. That realization is both freedom and happiness that no one can ever take from you. You have to know who you are, and accept yourself. Embrace your uniqueness and wear your imperfections like a crown. If you do, you will be admired for your individuality instead of judged for your shortcomings.

I fully understand that there are people in this world who will place judgement, and you need to understand that their judgements are reflections of how they feel about themselves. It has nothing to do with you. If you can get to that truth, and get past your feelings of not being good enough, they will have no power over you.

I have worked with people who have allowed their insecurities to get in the way of their successes, and in the way of their realizations of what they can bring to this world. I asked them all to identify the things they loathed, and then take the negative statements and turn them into positive ones. Affirmations are key to changing this mindset—and a mindset is all it is. It is a thought process that needs to be shifted. There are people every day who have surgeries to make themselves fit, when the beauty is that there is no requirement in the first place.

We live in a world where we are so obsessed with how we look on the outside that we forget to focus on our insides. Age is something that you cannot avoid, but wisdom is most often overlooked. Be wise, and embrace who you are. Do not worry for one more moment that you are not enough. You are beautiful just the way you are. If you do have fitness goals however, keep working towards them. Feeling good is the key to a happy life, and I am not advising you to stop focusing on health, and start on the Coke and Cheetos diet, but I am telling you that if you cannot love yourself in a size sixteen, you will not love yourself in a size eight. Tackle the underlying insecurities, and love yourself. If it takes saying it in the mirror every morning, do it. You cannot spend another moment not feeling good enough.

Build Your Army

It's not about quantity, it's about quality. If life is a battle, who do you want fighting beside you? Everyone should have people to turn to in moments when they need a connection, an ear, or some emotional support. Women especially need other women, yet we live in a world where women are more competitive than supportive. Love, real love, removes that competition. After you learn to love yourself, you have to be able to love others.

Some might argue that a support system isn't necessary, but I do not agree. In order to live a fulfilling life, you need relationships with people who matter. Cathy Williams states "Giving and receiving support from others is a basic human need." In the article *Importance of Developing a Support*

System, published December 10, 2014, she explains that support systems are key to getting through the ups and downs of life. We need people who understand us, and listen to us, while providing honest feedback. Not only does having a support system help you to enjoy life, but research has proven that it helps prevent depression and anxiety.

I want to make it very clear that there is a difference between a friend, and a person who plays a supporting role in your life. If you have a hard time identifying the difference, think through some of these questions.

1. **Looking at my circle of friends and family, who can I say loves me unconditionally?** Unconditional is the key here. Who in your life loves you without expectation? Who is always there with a helping hand,

regardless of the bad decisions you have made in your life? When Negative Nelly is in your head, whispering sweet nothings about your imperfections, who is there to counter the attack? My mom has always been my go-to person. That woman would help me bury a body. She'd bring the shovel and explain how it was the victim's fault. I can't make this up people. She has seen me at my worst. She has always brushed my hair back, wiped away the tears, and promised a better tomorrow, with an honesty that was just as harsh as it was kind at times. Who is that person for you?

2. **Who can I trust?** There is nothing worse than sharing pieces of yourself with others who take them for granted, or who love your story more than they love you. Who cares more about you than they care about the next big story? Over the years, I have had instances

where I have felt that a trusting friend was hard to find. But the friends I can trust go a long way, and they were worth finding.

3.   Who makes me feel good about myself?

Everyone has had a friend junk punch them in the name of honesty. Constructive honesty goes a long way if you want a real support system, but you don't need this person's honesty about how you are not doing what they think you should—all the while their own life is a train wreck. Hint: These people cannot see past their own judgements well enough to make the cut. Be friendly with them if necessary, but do not look to them to be part of your success plan.

4.   Do I feel uplifted when I spend time with these people? Pay attention to how you feel when you are

with certain people in your life. Look for warning signs, and know how to avoid the danger. If you do not feel peaceful or uplifted when you are around the people closest to you, it is time for you to create better circles. Being involved in Reiki and energy work over the years, I have learned that every interaction you have with other people is an energy transference. You give and take energy with everyone who crosses your path, and if you allow it, you make connections that can take from you more than they give. There are wonderful exercises you can do to cut the cords that bind you to those people, and if you feel that you are experiencing this I recommend that you seek out an energy healer to put you in a better place.

5.   Aside from feeling good around these people, do they make me happy? Relationships should bring you joy. They should be the icing on the cake, the spice

of life, and every other cheesy saying you can think of.

If you have valuable relationships with people, they

provide a lot fun and pleasure. You have to be happy

with the people you surround yourself with.

6.   Fill in this number with any other questions you

can think of, that will allow you determine who your

support system is. This is your life, and your story. Take

the time to identify what you need, in order to grow and

feel good about the people you choose to be your army

in the battle for your own success.

Say Goodbye to the Wrong People

Being an energy healer and a coach, I have always been a person who others turn to in times of need. I always call myself an energy docking station, and picture something from *Battlestar Galactica*. People have confided in me all my life, and have looked to me for counsel, advice, support, and unconditional love. I am the person who gets calls at one in the morning when my friends are having troubles, because they know I will be there. I support without judgment, and I ask honest, heartfelt questions to help people work through their situations.

After I started my coaching business, I discussed with a friend how I had been a coach for years, but I was now charging for it. Although this was said in jest at the time, it is true. I have a genuine desire to help make the world a better place, and to help others explore the beauty of their own lives. That being said, I feel that this is perhaps the most difficult and most important chapter to share with all of you. You wouldn't keep rotten food in your fridge, so why would you keep rotten people in your life? Rotten or toxic people depend on your support, friendship, and love, at the cost of draining you, and allowing you to give all that you have for their benefit. Not only are the wrong people in your life zapping your energy, they can actually be toxic to your progression and keep you away from the happiness you deserve.

A couple of years ago I had the opportunity to meet one of the most toxic people I have ever met. He hid his manipulation tactics well, and I realized I was far more concerned for his well-being than he was for anyone else's. A few months later I had the opportunity to spend some time with someone who he had kept in a very toxic

relationship for years. As this person shared truths about

her friend, I was appalled at the deception and behaviors

they both had allowed to continue. I set my personal

thoughts aside as I listened to her share some of the most

shocking stories. When we parted ways after our meeting, I

told her that I truly hoped she would love herself enough

to realize that she deserved better, and I was thankful that

her honesty prevented me from falling into anything

further. I walked away unharmed, but her relationship had

destroyed her self-worth and self-respect. It made me

question how we allow these things to happen in our lives,

and what we can do to prevent toxic people from

destroying all of the beauty in life, and therefore give

ourselves a chance to be free. It is not your responsibility to

fix everyone that is broken, but you do have an obligation

to protect yourself from the ones who cannot fix

themselves. When you allow toxicity, it deteriorates the relationships you have with everyone else who cares for you. Separating you from your loved ones, and allowing for alienation, is a key tactic for narcissistic people, and it will destroy your heart and soul.

Keeping these people around is perhaps the most serious of all errors you can make that will impede your chance for happiness. You will feel drained and lost. You will be tossed and turned in the throes of their chaotic behaviors, while they claim that you are the one accountable for the outcome. There is no responsibility you can take that will help buffer the actions taken by people that will use you for their own validation or personal gain.

I hope that I have your attention. Like many of you, I have had friends who were grandfathered in. One in particular, I had been friends with for twenty years. She and

I were kids when we met, and we had amazing,

adventurous stories, from trips we had taken and from

crazy antics. We worked together for a few years in our

twenties, and over time had become more like sisters than

friends. I knew that she pulled a lot of my energy, but she

and I had such a history that I didn't dare sever those ties. I

was convinced that she needed me and I wasn't going to

abandon her to face her chaos alone. I could handle it.

Our friendship consisted of me listening, and being

there for her, over and over again. I was happy to do it. We

had history, and she was having a rough go at life. She

would call all hours of the day and night, and would

repeatedly call or text until I answered. I started to realize

how exhausted I was becoming as her pillar of strength.

This was going to get better right? She did get better for a

while, and I knew she was better because I no longer heard

from her. She was happy, and things were going great. I

would try to check in with her and there was never a response. Holidays, birthdays, seasons all passed, and there was no contact. Then one night I received a call. She was down and needed my help again. I realized after that two-hour conversation where I listened to her cry and scream about the heartbreak she was experiencing (at one in the morning, during a work week), that I couldn't do it anymore. This was a person who was in her own world, and only needed me when she needed a recharge. She needed my strength when she couldn't make it on her own. She knew nothing about what was going on in my life. In fact, she would never ask about anything in my world at all. She didn't care enough to even try. I called our conversations drive-by dumpings. She would fly low, drop all of her feelings, and pull out.

I had begun to recognize what a toxic person looks like, and I knew that I needed to do something to protect myself. That led me down the path of learning to identify toxic behaviors, and learning to look for signs in any relationship, so that this wouldn't continue to happen. So how do you identify toxic people in your life?

1. **Are you the only emotional support for someone?** Has this person alienated everyone else in their lives? Are you the only person they lean on when things fall apart? Toxic people do not have many friends, so when they find someone that they can use as their docking station, they hold on for dear life.

2. **Do you keep their secrets?** Do they have hidden aspects of their lives that are your responsibility to protect? You may be in a

relationship with a toxic person if you feel the need to hide that relationship. That person is making poor decisions, and pulling you into their drama. A non-toxic person does not hide like a toxic person does. They are open and forthcoming, and expect their friends and relationships to be built on honesty and integrity.

3.   **Are you constantly defending them to other people who care for you?** If everyone else in your life has the same opinion of how this person treats you, or thinks that your relationship is unhealthy, then listen. Darlin' if it walks and looks like a duck, it's a duck.

4.   Are moments that you spend with this person always clouded with drama, guilt, shame, or sadness? Do you get pulled into the other person's drama and problems, and feel negative after any time that you spend with them? The relationships you have in your life should be uplifting, and bring joy. No friends should ever make you feel poorly about yourself, or the relationships you have with them.

5.   Do they lie to you? Run from liars. Don't fall for the person with the big story and no action. When a person is honest, their actions and words run parallel. You will believe what they say because they do what they say.

6.   Is this person always a victim? Are you dealing with someone who always has something happening to them? Their spouse doesn't love them; their dog kicks them when they come home from work? Someone is, and has always been taking from them, and you need to be there to pick up the pieces, right? Having a friend who is accountable for their life and their choices makes all the difference. Everyone has good and bad experiences, but if a person is in the midst of always being a victim, how long before it's their own fault?

7.   Do they make you feel manipulated, or bad about yourself? Welcome to a toxic person's power play. If you can spend your time feeling bad about something, you will be more responsive and willing to sacrifice for them. You, my friend, have become the second crab in their bucket, and they will use

their claws to keep you there.

**8.   Do they speak poorly of others and feel

they deserve special treatment?** This person is

always saying something bad about someone else.

You hear it every time you talk to them. They feel

that they are superior, and deserve special treatment,

while others just don't make the cut. If they are

talking about everyone else to you, how do you think

they talk about you to others? These behaviors are

consistent, and no one gets a free pass.

9.   Do they complain a lot? They always have a

tidbit of negativity to go with any glass of

champagne. They look for things to go wrong, and

they don't stop with the negative thoughts.

Negativity is draining, and if you will look at what it does to that person you will see how miserable toxic people are. How often do they smile or look alert? Do they ever look at the glass as half full, or is it always almost gone with nothing anywhere that could ever fill it again? When I think of this person, I hear the "Wicked Witch" song from the *Wizard of Oz* and see a pale moon rising. You get the picture.

10. Do they make you feel bad? Negative thoughts impede your spirit and your intuition. It is always cloudy for me when I spend time with a pessimist. I feel disconnected from my vibes for a bit, and have to work to regroup. When I was diagnosed with Celiac, I went to my doctor and his advice to me was that if a certain food made me sick,

I shouldn't eat it. My advice to you is that if a person makes you feel bad, you shouldn't spend time around them. It is always that simple.

My advice is to always walk away from toxic people; however that may not always be a possibility for you. If you have a person like this in your family, or work with someone who you feel drains you, the possibility to cut communication with them is not likely. I do have one word that I want to share, that will allow you to protect yourself. That word is *boundaries*.

Toxic relationships thrive when there are no boundaries. You have to be strong enough to take a stand for yourself, to protect your best interests and your heart. Referring back to the experience with my toxic friend, and the impact she had on my life, I realized that I needed to set parameters for myself that would protect me when I felt that I was being taken advantage of. I started with small things, like turning the ringer off on my phone before going to bed. I kept my work phone on, and shared that number with people in case of emergencies. When I did talk to her, I stopped giving advice, and started asking more questions to put decisions and reactions in her court. I stopped reaching out to her, and I stopped listening for countless hours when she called. I set the expectation that I had about fifteen or twenty minutes to chat with her before I had something I needed to do. I proactively shared what was going on in my world, instead of waiting for her to ask. When she shared something negative, I countered with something positive. Slowly, the calls started to die off. The last time I talked to her was when something truly terrible had happened in her life. I had heard from a friend that she was going through a tragedy, and when she called I offered my support, and told her how sorry I was. I asked if there was anything I could do to help her or her family, and something snapped. She got off the phone and removed me from her social media account, and that was it. We never spoke again. I am not sure what triggered that response, but I did not fight it. I came to terms with the fact that it was time to close that door, and move past a friendship that hadn't been healthy for years. It was over.

I have fallen into potentially toxic relationships since then, but my ability to remove myself has gained precision. Toxic people want you to feel sorry for them. It is perhaps the strongest way they pull compassionate people into their webs. Here are some suggestions that will help you protect yourself.

1.   When someone is complaining, or falling into victim status, use words of encouragement that will keep the responsibility on their side.
Ask more about how they will handle the situation

than how the situation makes them feel. It's okay to ask what they will do to resolve the issue. Remember that if this person is toxic, they don't want resolution, they want to be the victim. This will allow you to listen without putting any energy into solving problems for them, or taking on any of their responsibility.

2. **Avoid taking what they say personally.** If you are going to maintain a relationship with a toxic person, you can't allow what they say to hurt you. When you feel that you are being pulled in, or you start to feel inadequate or guilty, step back, take a deep breath, and consider the source. Perspective will clear your mind.

3.   You don't have to answer the phone. Decide

how you will handle communication. Is this

someone you have to keep in touch with? Can you

minimize contact with them? If you work with them,

never entertain outside of work. There is not a rule

that says you have to keep in contact with someone

who harms your spirit.

**4.   Spend time with people who have the same

goals, and visions of life that you do.** Choose

your friends wisely. If you find people with similar

thoughts and beliefs, the chance of attracting

someone who is toxic will decrease tremendously.

5.   Walk away from toxic people. If you cannot

set boundaries properly to protect yourself, you owe

it to yourself to remove the situation. Toxic people will make you sick. There is no rebound for you when you allow it to go too far. You will lose yourself, and that is not what you were born to do. Love yourself more than the façade that a toxic person presents to you, and go. Get out.

Every experience is an opportunity for you to grow. The relationships you have teach you what you want, and sometimes they teach you what you don't want. Treasure the moments you have either way, because they make you the person that you are.

Karri J. McClure

There Is No Such Thing as Wasted Time

Well baby, there you stand
With your little head, down in your hand
Oh, my God, you can't believe it's happening again
Your baby's gone, and you're all alone
And it looks like the end

And you're back out on the street
And you're tryin' to remember
How do you start it over
You don't know if you can
You don't care much for a stranger's touch
But you can't hold your man

You never thought you'd be alone
This far down the line
And I know what's been on your mind
You're afraid it's all been wasted time

The autumn leaves have got you thinking
About the first time that you fell
You didn't love the boy too much, no, no
You just loved the boy to well, farewell

So you live day to day
And you dream about tomorrow, oh
And the hours go by like minutes
And the shadows come to stay
So you take a little something
To make them go away
I could have done so many things, baby
If I could only stop my mind
From wonderin' what I left behind

And from worrying 'bout this wasted time

Ooh, another love has come and gone
Ooh, and the years keep rushing on
I remember what you told me before you went out on your own
Sometimes to keep it together, we got to leave it alone

So you can get on with your search, baby
And I can get on with mine
And maybe someday we will find
That it wasn't really wasted time

-The Eagles (Hotel California -1976)

This haunting song by Glen and Don was the song

that I made my theme song for the majority of my thirties.

I was sure that my life had started years before, and that

wasted time with the wrong guy, or the wrong job, or the

wrong situation, had left me on the sidelines. There was no

way a coach was going to put me in the game. I was sure

that I needed to throw in the towel and just exist. I was so

busy looking back at "wasted time," and thinking about

decisions gone terribly wrong, that I forgot to look at the

person I was becoming. Every situation and decision has helped me to become the person that I am. In the moment that I shifted my thoughts from dreaming about tomorrow to closing the door on the past and walking away, something happened. I started to remember who I was, and what I wanted, and I started to smile more. I was no longer on the sideline of my own life. I was falling and sliding all through that muddy game.

Conclusion

Well here we are at the end of our time together. There have been both joyful and tearful moments as I have shared all that I have. To open up and write so many personal experiences is hard to describe. I want to thank you for taking the time to read my book, and I hope that you have pulled something from it that will help you find your happiness.

If I could share anything else it would be the knowledge that you are loved, and that I wrote this book for you. I want you to find your happiness, because you deserve it. Imagine if we lived in a world where everyone chose joy; imagine if we were surrounded by people in pursuit of their dreams on a regular basis.

Believe in yourself, and trust that you can do anything you set out to do. Do not spend one more day waiting until tomorrow, when you can start today. I promise that you will be a better person for it. Share the beauty of who you are with people who deserve it, and be strong.

I hope you win.

Contact me:

Website: karrijmcclure.com

Email me directly: getoutandgethappy@gmail.com

Invictus

Out of the night that covers me,
Black as the Pit from pole to pole,
I thank whatever gods may be
For my unconquerable soul.

In the fell clutch of circumstance
I have not winced nor cried aloud.
Under the bludgeonings of chance
My head is bloody, but unbowed.

Beyond this place of wrath and tears
Looms but the Horror of the shade,
And yet the menace of the years
Finds and shall find me unafraid.

It matters not how strait the gate,
How charged with punishments the scroll
I am the master of my fate:
I am the captain of my soul.

-William Ernest Henley

ABOUT THE AUTHOR

Karri is a certified life coach and Reiki master. She lives on a ranch just outside of Phoenix, Arizona with her 3 crazy dogs. When Karri isn't helping people live happier lives, she is out camping, traveling, and seeking adventure with her dear family and friends. Karri studied at Southwest Institute of Healing Arts and is currently working on her next book.

Made in the USA
San Bernardino, CA
17 September 2018